THE UNDERDOG CODE

IMO ENANG

THE UNDERDOG CODE

Position yourself to win today and tomorrow

IMO ENANG

The Underdog Code
Copyright © 2023 Imo Enang
First published in 2023

Print: 978-1-76124-104-8
E-book: 978-1-76124-106-2
Hardback: 978-1-76124-105-5

All rights reserved. No part of this book may be reproduced, stored in a retrieval system, or transmitted by any means (electronic, mechanical, photocopying, recording, or otherwise) without written permission from the author.

Because of the dynamic nature of the Internet, any web addresses or links contained in this book may have changed since publication and may no longer be valid. The information in this book is based on the author's experiences and opinions. The views expressed in this book are solely those of the author and do not necessarily reflect the views of the publisher; the publisher hereby disclaims any responsibility for them.

The author of this book does not dispense any form of medical, legal, financial, or technical advice either directly or indirectly. The intent of the author is solely to provide information of a general nature to help you in your quest for personal development and growth. In the event you use any of the information in this book, the author and the publisher assume no responsibility for your actions. If any form of expert assistance is required, the services of a competent professional should be sought.

Publishing information
Publishing and design facilitated by
Passionpreneur Publishing
A division of Passionpreneur Organization Pty Ltd
ABN: 48640637529

Melbourne, VIC | Australia
www.PassionpreneurPublishing.com

This book is dedicated to all those who have been doubted or disbelieved by others.

TABLE OF CONTENTS

Acknowledgements		ix
About the Author		xi
Introduction		xiii
Chapter 1	My Story	1
Chapter 2	Big Picture — Prepare for a Mindset Shift	9
Chapter 3	The Power of Perception — How Your Outlook Can Change Your Outcome	21
Chapter 4	Who in the World Is an Underdog?	49
Chapter 5	The Underdog Doesn't Play Fair	71
Chapter 6	The Underdog Pivots	89
Chapter 7	The Underdog Has the 'Not Yet' Mindset	103
Conclusion: The Underdog Stays Hungry		129
Further Reading and Resources		135

ACKNOWLEDGEMENTS

I would like to acknowledge every single person out there who has supported me on my journey, from my dear family to my schoolmates, as well as my colleagues at work, my mentors, and my sponsors.

With you, I keep learning, unlearning, and re-learning – the game of life.

ABOUT THE AUTHOR

Imo is a broad skilled C-Suite Executive with several years of working experience across multiple industries like FMCG, Management Consulting, Banking and Academia. Holding multiple nationalities; Imo has had the privilege to live, work and study in Africa, Asia, UK and the EU, giving him a diverse view and a unique appreciation of multicultural profiles.

With an MBA from IE Business School, Madrid, he is currently studying a Doctorate in Strategy at Warwick Business School (UK) and has a Chartered Manager qualification from The Institute of Managers & Leaders (Australia & New Zealand). He is also a Lean Theory practitioner.

Imo is passionate about inspiring young professionals to middle-level managers to achieve their goals. He is a Success Principles Coach (Canfield Training Group) as well as a certified NLP (Neuro-Linguistic Programming) Mind Mastery trainer.

He is also the author of an International Best-Selling Book 'Don't Set Goals … Achieve Them!'

INTRODUCTION

What if I told you something?

The same 'disadvantages' that appear to limit your progress could be the 'unfair advantages' that can position you for continued success.

I'm talking about the Underdog state of mind, about the ultimate blueprint that can ensure that you win, not just today, but also tomorrow.

I'm referring to a state of mind where you have nothing to lose; where all you have is all you need and there's only one voice in your head telling you, 'I have what it takes to get to the top of that hill'.

A set of principles that guarantee that you're not the wolf on the hill, but rather the wolf climbing the hill.

Underdogs typically pull off surprising victories against their competitors — more often than you think. They do this by strategically neutralising the impact of their foes' capabilities.

Most of the opposition we face appears big, strong, and powerful but that doesn't matter as the Underdog won't engage in conventional combat — he would typically turn the combat on its head!

The Underdog goes against conventional wisdom and strategically alters the rules of engagement to neutralise his opponents' winning capabilities — his strength and his power. He renders his opponent irrelevant and flips the odds in his favour. In today's world, using strategy parlance, we can say that the Underdog typically embarks on a blue ocean shift (a market where you have little to no competition)!

When you compete in non-conventional ways … you will get laughed at or even criticised.

> 'First, they ignore you, then they laugh at you, then they fight you, then you win'.
>
> — Mahatma Gandhi

Fighting a battle on your terms means you need to have a deep understanding of the rules of engagement in a way that you can alter the rules to favour you.

When you doubt the Underdog, it's like music to their ears. You awaken an insatiable, unstoppable emotion in them, and *unleash* the lion inside them!

Tell me I'm not good enough,
tell me I'm not strong enough … tell me I won't finish!

They say you don't have what it takes to make that investment … they say you don't have what it takes to lose that weight … they say you don't have what it takes to succeed in that endeavour …

… These doubts are the fuel the Underdog needs to deliver. The Underdog converts that pain into propane!

This book is loaded with all the necessary blueprints to get you thinking, acting, and winning like the Underdog! Nine times out of ten, the Underdog comes out with the win because the Underdog is hungrier than the rest. The same way the wolf on the hill is never as hungry as the wolf climbing the hill!

What This Book Is Not About

Now, I'm sure you're ready to jump in, but before that, it's critical to state what this book is NOT about!

- A shortcut to getting things done with no work
- A set of items to enable you 'cut corners' and get results

- Principles you can read once and get absorbed in with very little effort

The bottom line is, no matter how fired up you are after reading this or any other self-help content, if you DO NOT put in the effort, if you DO NOT move, then absolutely NOTHING will move!

If you are a young adult, budding entrepreneur, fresh working-class entrant, junior or mid-level manager, or even a senior manager who wants a set of tested principles that guarantee sustainable success through evidence-based approaches, then this book is a great start.

Certainly, you will find the internet full of content on the Underdog and various other books in the market. While these may be helpful, this book uniquely unwraps the building blocks of an Underdog and reveals their historic winning strategies, distilling them down into actionable steps, with tools for implementation. This, therefore, is an holistic approach that is guaranteed to position you for that victory!

Essentially this book offers a blueprint to operate effectively as an Underdog and continually reap the Underdog's unfair advantages.

This disclaimer **informs readers that the views, thoughts, and opinions expressed in these texts belong solely to the**

author, and not necessarily to the author's employer, organisation, committee or any other group or individual.

Before we proceed any further, I would like to share a little of my story.

1

MY STORY

'The hardest walk you can make is the walk you make alone, but that is the walk that makes you the strongest'.

— Unknown

We've all been through tough times, regardless of how privileged or disadvantaged we may have been. These tough times could've been in the past, during our formative years, or later in life.

I recall not too long ago when I had to make a significant pivot in my career. Even though I thought I was ready, when it happened, it came so suddenly and jolted me off course for a while. But guess what? That was the beginning of incredible breakthroughs for me. There was a three-month window in which I went back to my drawing board and did a rigorous overhaul of my purpose (my passion, principles, and skill sets). I then visualised how I was going to create value for myself and the people around me by serving. I understood that serving the people around me, by being that inspiring conduit that motivates people to becoming the best version of themselves, was undoubtedly my calling.

But it wasn't easy, as I had to enter new spaces in my career; spaces that were out of my comfort zone and, for which, I had to learn, unlearn and re-learn. Looking back, it's evident that those few months of mental re-configuration were a stage. A stage that made me stronger and faster than ever before.

Basically, I became unstoppable!

Sometimes we need a dose of pain to prepare us for gain. From my elementary knowledge of medicine, I believe this is the principle that guides certain types of vaccines' functions. Let's look at a few basic principles of COVID-19 vaccines for a bit.

Without claiming to be a medical whiz (that's my way of laying a disclaimer!), let me tell you that the popular mRNA COVID-19 vaccine contains material from the virus that causes COVID-19 and it gives our cells instructions on how to make a harmless protein that is unique to the virus. After our cells make copies of the protein, they destroy the genetic material from the vaccine.

Our bodies recognise that this particular protein should not be there and they build T-lymphocytes and B-lymphocytes that will remember how to fight the virus that causes COVID-19 if we are infected in the future.

This is the same principle that comes through when we are faced with setbacks or failures. We're able to turn these events into *'vaccines'* when we maintain the right attitude that enable us to extract the learnings from those setbacks and bounce back even stronger.

Similar to the virulent material that causes COVID-19, the setbacks contain the smaller versions of major setbacks that could cripple us completely. However, once we surmount them, we are strengthened for anything in the future.

We become truly Unstoppable!

The hardest walk is often walking alone. But then again, it is foundational, and it determines how well and how far we will eventually go.

Underdogs understand this very well. They train themselves behind the scenes by stretching themselves to the limit so that when they show up in the world, they appear to flow seamlessly!

I considered numerous superstars from different endeavours and eras. In tennis, the very recent Emma Raducanu's unbelievable ascension to British #1 position; in business, Steve Jobs against all odds with Apple at the turn of the 21st Century; in music, Cher dubbed the 'queen of the comeback' ... the list is endless!

One commonality among all these superstars is that they practised extensively in the background and then arrived ready to the battleground. This unique Underdog characteristic bolsters that incredible *'can do attitude'* in Underdogs.

At the same time, the outside world would have written off the Underdog as they're not the favourites and they normally don't stand a chance, right? Well, nothing could be further from the truth!

This seemingly counterintuitive way of thinking is where Underdogs thrive. Underdogs leverage the ignorance of the masses about their subtle (and largely unnoticeable) unfair advantages.

One of the greatest Underdogs we will talk about later in this book is a character from the Bible — the story of David. David had practised and tested himself so many times behind the scenes with lions and bears that tried to ravage his flock. Only a few people knew this, so he had to remind the Israelites of his capability to take on the previously undefeated champ — Goliath the Giant!

I built a powerful belief system around the principles that govern the Underdog mindset, and it has enabled me to outperform the favourites in everything I have set out to achieve. I developed unique qualities and strengths only a few can admire, because most don't possess them and haven't experienced them.

I was able to do all of this because I knew the value of walking alone at strategic times — a critical feature of the Underdog. I understood how, and why David defeated the giant Goliath. I saw how the establishment of systems and structures could become the greatest leverage imaginable.

Now, let's look at the big picture to gain a bird's eye view of what you're going to read in this amazing book!

Ready,

Set,

Let's GO!

2

BIG PICTURE — PREPARE FOR A MINDSET SHIFT

'The Wolf on the hill is not as hungry as
the Wolf climbing the hill'.

— Arnold Schwarzenegger

We've probably heard several times that prior success may be a barrier to future success. The question is — why would something that should enable us to raise the bar of excellence anywhere, be the major deterrent to achieving, in some cases, even the same level of excellence?

I believe Myles Munroe summed it up well enough when he referred to our greatest enemy of progress as our last success.

This is because one may become so proud of what one has already accomplished and this may prevent one from pushing forward.

In this chapter, you will learn the major driver of the Underdog. You will understand that the Underdog mentality is the perfect mindset to ensure you program yourself to strive for continuous improvement in everything you do. This will set you on the track to adopt and adapt the Underdog Code regardless of your past or present experience of privilege or disadvantage.

What Economics Teaches Us

In elementary economics (and in marketing), we were taught the differences between a need, a want, and a demand. Our needs are channelled towards satisfying our basic requirements; our wants towards specific requirements (in marketing, wants are understood to be driven by our cultural or stereotypical influences); and our demands are our wants backed up by our willingness *and* ability to pay. So, until a desire is supported by the willingness and ability to pay, it remains just a desire and that's why we're told '*if wishes were horses, beggars would ride*'!

Similarly, success is sweet; it feels great to achieve your goals, right? It even becomes more interesting when you receive accolades after a success. But often, when success sets in and is assumed to be the destination instead of the journey, we fall into the trap of having a desire that isn't supported by the necessary criteria — a combination of willingness and ability to pay.

If we correlate success as a journey versus success as a destination, we see that the criteria that could make or break us in terms of delivering ongoing success would be the right hunger (in earlier example: willingness) and skill set (in earlier example: the ability to pay).

Mindset Shift

You're probably familiar with the phrase, 'the good old days' or 'back in the day'. These are often used to celebrate past victories. The question is, why were the old days better than today? Or why did you stop being the best? I'm not sure there's anyone who wants short lived success. Even in politics, you sometimes find an incumbent who doesn't want to give up the seat of power, even after promising to leave after a first term! When they eventually win their seat, they seem to forget everything or change their mind and embark on a second or third term. Some even go on to think it's their birthright! The point is that no one ever says, 'I just want to be successful for a brief period of time'.

However, to remain successful, we need to assume we never even succeeded! Our achievements need to be constantly viewed as building blocks; we must transition from being the wolf at the top of the hill to the wolf climbing the hill!

Big Picture (the How)

I still have a very clear image of a winning goal I scored in fifth grade when I played as a defender for my soccer team. I did some dribbles and came all the way from the defence to take an unexpected shot just after the midfield and, quite surprisingly to me, I secured an amazing goal!

FIG 1: CHAPTER ILLUSTRATION

I was insane with joy, my teammates were amazed, and I suddenly felt that my entire life was so sweet! I'm sure many of us can relate to the feeling … no one can easily forget a victory! Those times we've won, or come out on top, have remained etched in our minds. The winning moments are reels that automatically play several times, and we like to reflect on these to feel good about ourselves or to bolster ourselves in tough times.

Certainly, winning is great, but does it drive us to reflect internally on the drivers of that success and thus, improve ourselves overall? Often, when we succeed in an activity, we move on to the next almost automatically. Returning to my soccer experience, I can tell you that scoring that unexpected goal and helping my team win the match didn't compel me to re-evaluate my practice strategies because I instinctively believed I was 'the guy'. I had discovered the tricks and I was an expert, right? Or perhaps not.

Essentially, there was no need for me to continue practising for several hours or invite a friend to watch me as I constantly tried and tried again to perfect my skills. I didn't have to learn to identify my weak points or go through the journey of designing to fix the issues. I had won *and could keep winning*!

Let's try to flip this around a bit. What if I had actually lost and I missed the shot and dashed the hopes of my team members? What do you think? It may have turned out better for me. Don't get me wrong, it's indeed bliss to win and continue winning. But if we keep winning; how do we improve, learn, unlearn, and re-learn?

The problem is that we all have this protective impulse as human beings — the desire to refrain from challenges or anything that uproots us from our comfort zone. We love to win and to continue winning, and anything that interrupts this flow is counterintuitive.

The problem with constantly winning (without looking back to truly reflect on the fact that we're still 'trying to win') is that we're unable to truly confront our demons. The toughest times we've had would be those times when we contended with the storms of life. But then again, in these rare moments, we almost always see the silver lining. We typically come out stronger, with more ammunition, and are more resilient to turbulence in the future.

The people with the ability to look deep into themselves and identify ways to confront and learn valuable lessons from their failures without falling apart are the ones who will ultimately succeed. The question is: 'How would you learn from your mistakes if you never made any?'

Losing should be seen through the lens of pivoting. It's fine to lose and to lose again … but with every time you lose, you need to pivot. Pivoting here means picking yourself up from the floor when you fall, gathering lessons learned from the experience, and then re-applying them going forward.

The Underdog Hunger Is Insatiable

The greatest metaphor for success is hunger. The wolves that are still climbing are hungry for the 'food' at the top of the hill. Now, compare that with the wolves already at the top. These wolves have reached what they consider as the top of their game, and in their thinking, they no longer have the urge to seek greater heights. They place themselves in a complacent position — the perfect position for the Underdogs to overtake! Don't get me wrong! It's great to succeed, but once you do you need to walk back to the bottom of the hill and back into the Underdog mindset to guarantee momentum!

The Underdog Has Unfair Advantages

As expected, athletes want to win ... but in the quest to beat the opposition, they may become cunningly creative by altering the rules to their advantage all the time and thus, achieving unfair advantages.

A great example would be Tim Ferriss' Gold in the Chinese Kickboxing National Championships. At face value, this seemed impossible given the short time he had to prepare for the championships (only four weeks). Tim studied the rules and identified two loopholes.

First, he noticed that the weigh-ins that determine your competing category are done the day prior to the competition. Ferriss used dehydration techniques to lose 28 pounds and, immediately after the weigh-in, regained this weight again by 'hyper-hydration'. Using his words in his best-seller *The 4-hour Work Week*, Ferriss writes: 'It's hard to fight someone from three weight classes above you. Poor little guys'.

Secondly, Ferriss noticed that when one combatant falls off the elevated platform three times in a single round, his opponent will always win. Ferriss therefore channelled his efforts into pushing his opponents, instead of the conventional kicking and punching! The much heavier Ferriss (post his hyper-hydration) pushed his opponents from the platform three times in a row and won unconventionally ... but won nonetheless!

Another interesting twist to the rules of engagement was done by football legend Johan Cruijff in 1982. Cruijff scored an iconic goal in a way that completely surprised the goalkeeper!

Cruijff understood that the rules didn't prescribe that during a penalty, the ball had to be kicked directly at the goal. According to the rules, the ball just had to be played forward. Therefore, Cruijff leveraged the 'loophole' to his advantage by surprising the goalkeeper with a pass to his teammate instead of a direct kick at goal. This turned it into a 5 second gameplay with two strikers versus the extremely surprised goalkeeper, and resulted in a goal! Decades later, we saw how the trick was later recreated by Lionel Messi and Luis Suárez.

The Underdog Code

What if I told you there is a unique set of codified approaches that will guarantee you maintain the Underdog mindset regardless of where you are on the trajectory to success? What this means is that regardless of how many wins you had, you will still win today and win tomorrow! These codes ensure you continually take on the critical elements that places an Underdog well positioned to win. The Underdog Codes will help you rethink many aspects in your current journey, such as:

- What if I told you that certain things you have long seen as set-backs are truly set-forwards for your greatness?

- Imagine if the very things holding you down could be flipped 180°?
- How would you feel knowing that your current 'disadvantages' are actually your unfair advantages?

My goal here is to share from my experiences, and include insights I have gained over the years that cumulate into a blueprint I call the Underdog Codes.

The Underdog Codes comprise a toolkit of principles that will ensure you're constantly leveraging the Underdog mindset in all you do, and this will guarantee sustainable wins. We will look at these codes across the next five chapters of the book.

Now, let's explore the mind of an Underdog through the lens of the power of perception.

If you forget anything in the last chapter ...

don't forget this:

'All You Have Is Indeed All You Need!'

3

THE POWER OF PERCEPTION — HOW YOUR OUTLOOK CAN CHANGE YOUR OUTCOME

'Life is 10 percent what you make it,
and 90 percent how you take it'.

— Irving Berlin

Why are things generally not the way they appear at face value? Why would the same thing mean fundamentally different things even to people of similar backgrounds and paradigms? The power of perception grants answers to these questions. How you perceive things is an indicator of how you receive things. Perception is said to draw its roots from the Latin word *perceptio*, which means receiving or gathering.

By the end of this chapter, you will understand how critical our perceptions can be, and how they can become the focal point of inflection in our activity system. You will see the different possible combinations of relationships we can have based on different outcomes using *Jack Canfield's* E + R = O relationship. You will also learn how we can re-configure our perception to induce the right outcomes.

What's the Big Deal about Perception?

Think about a time when a seemingly negative event somehow turned around to be positive. Can you recall how things suddenly changed? Can you pinpoint the way you absorbed the initial event and the causal factors that influenced the changes that eventually happened? Chances are that the changes started from you. That's right — from you!

A while ago, when I was applying for my post graduate studies, I took the entry test and was confident that I would ace it. The results came through and I was told I was borderline and just managed to scrape through. This came as such a huge shock to me, but then I immediately interpreted it to mean that I was very fortunate to enjoy two things: firstly, I still scraped through the test and did not need to re-write it, and secondly, I got feedback early enough that I would need to significantly raise my standards to much higher levels as I commenced the program, and aim for the top percentile.

So rather than feeling sorry for myself, I was excited, and immediately began working on these two things. I ended up at the top of my class, turning 180° from where I was at the beginning, simply because of the way I perceived the feedback I got on my scores! That's one memorable point for me which I like to refer to when I need to 'program my software' (mind) accordingly. Now let's see how the power of perception radically changed things for someone decades ago during the Second World War.

Viktor Frankl, an Austrian neurologist, psychiatrist, philosopher, and globally recognised best-selling author, had spent three years during World War II living under extreme circumstances in Nazi concentration camps. Re-affirming to himself that he held the power to determine his response mechanism in view of the absolute horror that his new life had become, he chose to imagine being able to see his wife again. He even further imagined himself getting back to his daily beats and teaching his students about lessons he had learnt after the war was over.

> 'Between stimulus and response there is a space.
> In that space is our power to choose our response.
> In our response lies our growth and our freedom'.
>
> — Viktor Frankl

And so, he chose to imagine.

He imagined his wife and the prospect of seeing her again. He imagined himself teaching students after the war about the lessons he had learned. And just as his perceptions were, his reality became — Frankl was eventually able to recount his horrific experiences of living in the Nazi concentration camps as he survived the entire ordeal. Incredible! Frankl went on to publish numerous books selling millions of copies, amongst which was, 'Man's Search for Meaning', which he wrote in 1946, selling over 10 million copies.

Our Perception will either free us or cage us.

The Story of the Elephant Rope

FIG 2: THE STORY OF THE ELEPHANT

A man, walking through an elephant camp, spotted that the elephants were being restrained by unusual means — just a small piece of rope tied to one of their legs and affixed to a small stump in the ground. As the man gazed upon the elephants, he couldn't understand why the elephants wouldn't simply break the rope and escape the camp, since they are so strong. Curious, he asked a trainer nearby why the elephants never tried to escape. The trainer replied, *'when they were very young and much smaller, we used the same size and type of rope to tie them, and at that age it was sufficient to hold them. As they grew up, they became conditioned to believe they couldn't break away. Today, they're still bound by the thought that the rope can still hold them and so they remain captive in the camp'.*

Moral of the story: We can either remain bound by or be liberated from our thoughts and mental constraints. As one of my former bosses would say, 'It's in our hands!'

What Is Perception?

Wikipedia defines perception as 'the organization, identification, and interpretation of sensory information in order to represent and understand the presented information or environment'.

In addition to the recipient's learning, memory, expectancy, and attention; perception is the active interpretation of these signals. The process of sensory intake raises the level of this low-level information to that of higher-level information (e.g., extracts shapes for object recognition). The subsequent procedure links a person's concepts and expectations (or knowledge), restorative and selective mechanisms (like attention), and perception-influencing mechanisms.

All perception involves signals that go through the nervous system, that in turn result from physical or chemical stimulation of the sensory system. Vision involves light striking the retina of the eye; smell is mediated by odour; and hearing involves pressure waves.

> 'Whether you think you can or
> think you can't — you're right'.
>
> — Henry Ford.

A recent study revealed that 'one big difference between people who think intelligence is malleable and those who think intelligence is fixed is how they respond to mistakes'. This breakthrough study, conducted by Jason S. Moser of Michigan State University (with Hans S. Schroder, Carrie Heeter, Tim P. Moran, and Yu-Hao Lee), found that people who think intelligence is malleable say things like, 'when the going gets tough, I put in more effort' or 'if I make a mistake, I try to learn and figure it out'. Conversely, people who think that they can't get smarter will not take opportunities to learn from their mistakes. What this means is that the student who assumes their intelligence is capped or fixed may not think it makes sense to put in extra effort after failing a test.

> *It's never really about what happens to us,*
> *it's about how we happen to take It!*

During the study, Moser and his associates gave participants a task that is prone to error. The middle letter in a five-letter series, such as 'MMMMM' or 'NNMNN' had to be recognised by the participants. Sometimes the middle letter matched the other four, other times it didn't. Moser asserted that concentration occasionally drifts for no apparent reason, even when repeating the same behaviour. When this happens people make mistakes, but they realise quickly and then feel stupid.

The study of electrical activity in the brain has shown that when someone makes a mistake, their brain quickly sends two signals: the first, known as the 'oh crap' response, and the second, more like an awakening response, which indicates the person is aware of the mistake and attempting to fix it. Both alerts appear within a quarter-second of the error. To determine if participants believed it was possible to learn from mistakes, the researchers examined their responses after the experiment.

People who believed they could learn from their mistakes performed better after making a mistake, and were more successful at recovering. According to Moser, their brains also reacted differently, creating a stronger version of the second signal, which reads, *'I see that I've made a mistake, so I should pay more attention'*.

'Based on the findings, these individuals differ fundamentally from one another', Moser claims. This sheds light on the reasons why the two groups of people react differently to mistakes. According to Moser, people who believe they can learn from their failures have brains that are wired to focus more on errors. By demonstrating how the brain responds to errors, this research may aid in teaching people to feel that they can work harder, learn more, and improve themselves.

Your outlook determines your outcome.

The Power of Perception: Thinking Makes It So

One of my favourite stories is an ancient Chinese fable about a farmer in a small village.

FIG 3: OLD CHINESE FABLE 'GOOD LUCK BAD LUCK WHO KNOWS?'

A farmer and his son had a beloved horse who helped the family to earn a living. One day, the horse ran away and their neighbours exclaimed, 'Your horse ran away, what terrible luck!' The farmer replied, 'Maybe so, maybe not'. A few days later, the horse returned home, leading a few wild horses back to the farm as well. The neighbours shouted out, 'Your horse has returned, and brought several horses home with him. What great luck!' The farmer replied, 'Maybe so, maybe not'.

Later that week, the farmer's son was trying to ride one of the horses and she threw him to the ground, breaking his leg. The neighbours cried, 'Your son broke his leg, what terrible luck!' The farmer replied, 'Maybe so, maybe not'.

A few weeks later soldiers from the national army marched through town, recruiting all boys for the army. They did not take the farmer's son, because he had a broken leg. The neighbours shouted, 'Your boy is spared, what tremendous luck!' To which the farmer replied, 'Maybe so, maybe not. We'll see'.

> 'There is nothing either good or bad
> but thinking makes it so'.
>
> — William Shakespeare, Hamlet

This fable of the farmer is confusing at first. It clashes with the common belief that life's events carry intrinsic meaning.

Most people think of events in this way: *'certain things are good, and other things are bad. That's just the way they are'*.

A direct relationship exists between the event and your response.

Most people expect their outcome as a straight-line projection of the event. Usually this is incorrect, as we have the ability to change the outcomes we receive based on what we perceive.

The Chinese fable helps to express this in a clearer way.

How People Perceive Events Unfold

FIG 4: CHAPTER ILLUSTRATION

Oftentimes, we assume a straight-line connection between events. Imagine, for instance, that a man has just been told that his bid on a contract fell through; he interprets this as a bad thing and responds negatively. But as the fable illustrates, the link between an event and your experience is not so cut-and-dry. Rather, insights and studies have shown that your internal representation of life's events indicates how you perceive and react to them, and what the outcome will be. For a certain event, therefore, there may be different ways we internalise and interpret the outcome.

How Events Unfold

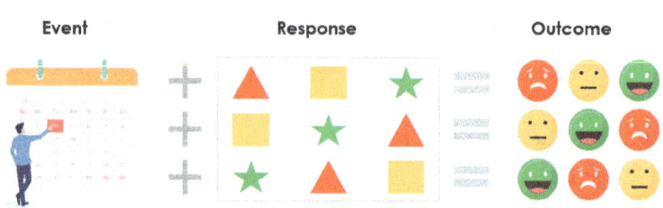

FIG 5: CHAPTER ILLUSTRATION

E + R = O (*Using Jack Canfield's popular equation to express the relationship between Events, Responses, and Outcomes*)

The fable of the Chinese farmer gives us an example of this in action. While the neighbours were swept up in the automatic judgements about what is good and bad, the farmer was careful not to be swayed easily or led astray by the events unfolding in his life. He knew that every event in life has multiple possible interpretations.

The key message here is that **since life's events aren't imbued with universal meaning, *you* get to select how you feel about things**. So, basically ***you* are in control of your own life's narrative**.

Re-Writing the Narrative

> 'If life hands you some crappy chapters ...
> then rewrite your Story'.
>
> — Ireland Gill

You can re-write the narrative and change everything! In fact, you are the author of your story and so if you're stuck on the same page, remember that at any moment in time, you hold the power to write a brand-new chapter.

You can select the right narrative by programming your perception and arriving at favourable outcomes.

32 THE UNDERDOG CODE

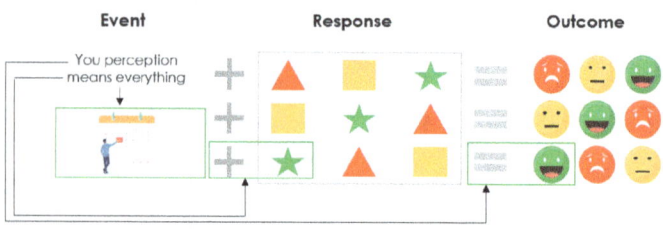

FIG 6: CHAPTER ILLUSTRATION

Note carefully: This isn't daydreaming about things that are inconsistent with reality — quite far from it. Nor is it brainwashing ourselves to simply embrace only positives by being impractical. This is about the clear philosophy that nothing is fixed in life. Life is completely dynamic, as we see in the phenomenon of change. Change is constant; change is a way of life. Therefore, our perception influences our narrative, which in turn, influences our outcomes. We have absolute control over our perception and thus, absolute control over our narratives, which means at the end of the day, our circle of influence will eventually extend to our outcome.

Two Sides to Everything on This Planet

Everything on this planet is dual by design as it's improbable for a thing to exist with only one side. For instance, you have two sides to a coin, two sides to a slice of bread, etc. In the same way, there are two sides to your view of an event. There will always be at least two ways you can interpret and respond to an event

THE POWER OF PERCEPTION 33

which ultimately affects the outcome. Hold this thought as we continue.

We all have seen a painting for example. Have you ever wondered why the painting is typically put in a frame? The frame enables you to focus more on the painting. The frame allows you to channel your attention onto the painting. This is what happens when we decide to settle for a particular response mechanism. If we decide to interpret an event as a negative one, we will place a frame of negativity around that event and so our response will then generate negative energy as we focus on negativity (thanks to the frame we placed on it).

You may be wondering, 'how would a simple thought generate energy, and negative energy for that matter?' I have pondered on this for a few years, and come up with two simple interrelated reasons (one contingent on the other). Energy is neither created nor destroyed (First Law of Thermodynamics); this means that the total energy of a system remains constant, even if it is converted from one form to another (Zohuri, 2018). As humans, we exude energy and as such, even our thoughts release energy behind the principle of the law of attraction. Remember the phrase 'e-motion' as 'Energy-in motion'? When we amplify our thoughts, we tend to convert energy through emotions … through energy-in-motion!

Your focus (amplified by your frame) is a conversion of energy via your 'type' of vibration (which could be positive or negative). So, when you have doubts, you are drained of energy as you're expecting an unfavourable outcome! Conversely, when you anticipate a positive outlook, you're energised by focusing on the positive and in turn, you bounce off even more positive energy, which ultimately affects the outcome of an event, making it skewed to a positive outcome! Basically, in one response mechanism, you're shedding off energy; in another, you're energised!

If only we knew how much control we have over events that happen to us, we would spend more time extracting the positive parts.

Now, recall the thought I asked you to hold on to for a second? Let's get back to it! We said everything has two sides, right? So, every event has two possible responses. Let's double down on that a bit more. This means that for every event, whether good or bad, there is a good and bad way to respond. Again, let's refer to elementary physics. Newton's Third Law of Motion, the Law of Action & Reaction, says:

'For every action, there is an opposite and equal reaction'.

If for example, I hit someone on the road while rushing in my car to catch a flight for which I was tracking to be 10 minutes late … it means there will be a positive side to this as well as a negative side to it. Right? Yes, for sure!

What Could the Positive Side Be?

Due to the car accident, the fact that I may then have to cancel my flight and spend a little more time with my daughter who had complained that she really wanted me to take her to the park the next day (and I was probably pushing it for the 5th time in a row!). Or that I had the opportunity to make a new friend who I realised has very similar interests to me and we could explore other businesses together? Or maybe the extra 'created time' I had, given I wouldn't be able to travel anymore, so I could spend the time working on my book and completing a report I had been putting aside (of course, all of these would come after taking my daughter out to the park).

The list goes on and on and on.

On the Other Side, the Negatives, Could Be

Due to the car accident, I missed my flight and now I would come across as highly disorganised to my clients who I was flying out to meet in the first place. How can a senior business executive who teaches and preaches on productivity have such a problem with coordinating himself for a flight? I would've lost momentum on the project I was to handle and this would set me back by at least two weeks. It may result in the project being overrun by time and cost, violating the basis upon which the project was allocated to me! This would create a negative spiral effect from penalties I would have to offset to my personal brand name being tainted.

I would also need to pay any extras that the car insurance may not cover due to my negligence … and hey, my car would be out of action for at least a week, and I would have to make do with moving around in a taxi for the next fortnight or so. Not convenient for me!

Now, we can see that we can internalise the same event, in different ways based on our filters and our response mechanisms. But here's the thing:

> 'Where focus goes, energy flows'.
>
> — Tony Robbins

So, if I fan the flames of negativity, I would invite doubts, transferring and squandering energy by vibrating negative energy as I expect a negative outcome!

On the other hand, if I fan the flames of positivity, I'm creating more and more anticipation, which attracts energy to me as I, in turn, vibrate with positivity in anticipation of a favourable outcome.

Most likely, we have no control over the facts, but we DO have incredible control over our response to those facts, and this ultimately affects the outcome!

How Can We Manage Our Narrative?

In a study conducted in 2010, Harvard psychologists Matthew Killingsworth and Daniel Gilbert recorded details of what 2,250 participants' minds were focused on with respect to what they did and what they felt. Their studies led to the interesting insight that each individual spends, on average, 47% of their day on 'autopilot'. This means almost half of the time; we do things without even consciously considering them. Science tells us that this happens when our basal ganglia (our subconscious brain) takes the lead ahead of our pre-frontal cortex (conscious brain).

FIG 7: CHAPTER ILLUSTRATION

This phenomenon could be responsible for an individual's hasty decision making, which is linked to their paradigms and re-enforced by the autopilot system. It follows that, to disrupt hasty, default, wrong perceptions, we need to intercept the regular neural pathway established by our autopilot mechanism.

We can alter the auto-pilot mechanism by adopting the mindfulness approach via meditation. Most of these default biases influencing our perceptions have been consolidated from childhood. However, they're not cast in stone and can be reprogrammed accordingly by mindfulness techniques. Developing mindfulness helps you *notice* when your automatic responses are kicking in. It creates space between events and your reactions. So, by cultivating regular states of mindful awareness (e.g., meditation), you build the capacity to control your narrative.

A Personal Experience

I went to a boarding school during my high school days and initially struggled to respond to the siren that directed my days. Usually as a junior student you would get punished for missing these deadlines, so I became unknowingly configured to prioritise speed over quality as I would recall the punishments for not 'meeting' deadlines, even two decades after I graduated from high school!

But by understanding that my autopilot is to prioritise speed, I can establish a maker/checker principle where I always go back to ensure I have delivered an activity with quality, and have not simply rushed through to tick the box.

I have been able to do this by deploying the mindfulness principle and pausing to audit my actions accordingly.

Perception Means Positioning: How Optical Illusions Cause Us to Position Things Differently

I have always been amazed at how our eyes, which we trust significantly, may so easily succumb to optical illusions. This is another aspect of life that shows that what we perceive determines how we position things.

The renowned experimental psychologist Tom Cornsweet, who first described optical illusions in the 1960s, depicts very clearly how our eyes can see and interpret things quite differently based on circumstances surrounding the visual activity.

Cornsweet discovered that people interpret colour and shade in 3D images differently depending on how an object is lit, and how shadows are cast. The impression is similar to another optical illusion called the checker shadow illusion created by Edward H. Adelson in the subsequent pages. Following this, will be an exercise to help us re-write our narrative as we converge to see what we have learnt from the chapter so far.

FIG 8: CHAPTER ILLUSTRATION. SOURCE: TOM CORNSWEET

40 THE UNDERDOG CODE

Depending on how an object is lit and how shadows are cast, humans have different perceptions of shade in 3D images.

Given that the two blocks are slanted away from us and the light is coming from the Upper left corner of the image, we will see the higher block as illuminated and the lower block as in shadow.

When the two blocks are shaded differently, our brain sees the top block as dark and the bottom block as light. Because our minds anticipate that the upper square will be darker and the bottom one lighter based on the other elements surrounding the grey, we interpret the higher square to be darker.

To verify this, run a finger down the middle of the line separating the darker and lighter areas; then the true colours will be visible.

FIG 9: SHADOW OPTICAL ILLUSTRATION. SOURCE: EDWARD ADELSON

Shadow Optical Illusion

With the help of this amazing optical illusion, the brain is tricked into perceiving colours differently than how they truly are.

The above-mentioned illusion, and other potent optical illusions, serve as powerful reminders that despite evidence to the contrary, things are not always as they seem. Look at the hues of the squares below with the letters A and B. Do they match, or is one of them darker than the other?

The square A is often seen as being significantly darker than the square B.

Well, let's uncover the truth now!

Amazingly, they are the same. Let's prove it ... The evidence is in the picture below, but many people still ignore it.

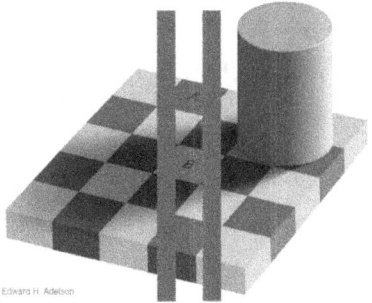

FIG 10: SHADOW OPTICAL ILLUSTRATION. SOURCE: EDWARD ADELSON

42   THE UNDERDOG CODE

The brain has trouble accepting what it is witnessing. This optical trick highlights the need of relativity in measuring objects as well as the effects of perception, in this case, light and shadow.

The way we view something affects what we see. Values are determined by perspective and relativity. Absolutes are uncommon in everyday life. A person's perspective and the context in which something exists determine how relative most things are.

To emphasise this further, here is a duplicate of the illusion:

FIG 11: SHADOW OPTICAL ILLUSTRATION. SOURCE: EDWARD ADELSON

Full credits for these optical illusion images go to Edward Adelson of The Department of Brain and Cognitive Sciences at Massachusetts Institute of Technology. Edward is the John and Dorothy Wilson Professor of Vision Science.

Exercise I — Re-Writing Your Narrative

Here's a simple 5-point process for re-writing your narrative

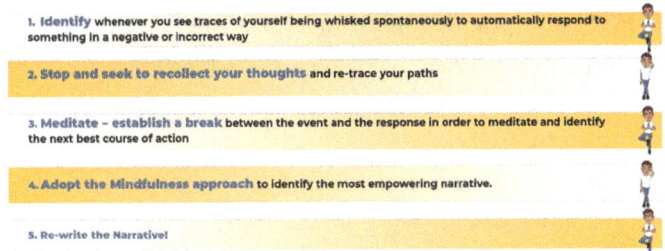

1. **Identify** whenever you see traces of yourself being whisked spontaneously to automatically respond to something in a negative or incorrect way

2. **Stop and seek to recollect your thoughts** and re-trace your paths

3. **Meditate** – establish a break between the event and the response in order to meditate and identify the next best course of action

4. **Adopt the Mindfulness approach** to identify the most empowering narrative.

5. **Re-write the Narrative!**

Exercise II — Sample Changes

Here are a few examples to illustrate how this might work in different parts of your life.

- **At work you're assigned a task that you do not enjoy doing.**
  Automatic Reaction: *Why am I assigned this task? They know I do not enjoy doing this task but keep passing it on to me. They want me to fail!*
  Choosing the Empowering Narrative: Oh great! At least I get another chance to figure out why I don't like this task, and fix that.
- **There's a child crying beside you.**
  Automatic Reaction: *Why is this child disturbing my peace? I cannot concentrate with this distraction!*

Choosing the Empowering Narrative: Here's an opportunity to put a smile on a child's face and do some good.

- **You just missed the bus.**

  Automatic Reaction: *Why am I always so late? I just can't do anything on time.*

  Choosing the Empowering Narrative: Well, I get some extra time to listen to that podcast or think about the book I have read recently and have a chance to reflect before the next bus arrives.

- **You missed a day of workout.**

  Automatic Reaction: *I knew working out was just not for me, I'm done.*

  Choosing the Empowering Narrative: Today was not quite as I expected so I couldn't workout. Tomorrow I will make up for lost time.

- **You're walking home from work and a thunderstorm catches you by surprise.**

  Automatic Reaction: *Rain is not good! Getting wet is uncomfortable! This is bad!*

  Choosing the Empowering Narrative: That was unexpected! Now that I'm all wet, I realise it's actually pretty calming and refreshing to be outside in a storm! My clothing gets wet in the wash anyway. It'll all dry off when I'm home.

- **You felt great about your performance in a job interview but don't get hired for the job.**

  Automatic Reaction: *That sucks! I really wanted that job. Maybe I'm no good at this after all.*

  Choosing the Empowering Narrative: It must not have been a mutual fit! If that's the case, I probably wouldn't have enjoyed working there as much as I thought I would. Now I can find a job that's truly aligned with my values and interests!

- **It's your night to cook dinner, and just when it's ready, your partner calls and says they'll be an hour late.**
  Automatic Reaction: *How disrespectful! Don't they know how hard I worked to make this meal? And the food's going to be cold!*
  Choosing the Empowering Narrative: That's no big deal, the food will stay warm in the oven. I can use this time to read that book I've been meaning to start.

Use the Power of Perception to Live Your Best Life

'Our life is what our thoughts make it'.

— Marcus Aurelius, Meditations

Life really is what you make of it.

What Did We Learn?

We started this chapter by explaining the importance role perception plays in the eventual outcome of events that affect us. We saw how the way we perceive things is indeed the way we receive things and that can largely impact the outcome based on Jack Canfield's powerful relationship O = E + R, where the Outcome is a function of the Event in addition to your response to the Event. We further explored how we can re-write our narrative by adopting the right response to events and sustainably change the outcome to our desired outcome. Finally, we saw how to leverage our automation machine to drive the right responses and deliver on our expected outcomes.

What's Next?

Now that we're clear on the impact of context and the art of positioning based on our perceptions, we will get into the main frame of the book by exploring the Underdog mindset and how that can truly position an individual to win.

If you forget anything in the last chapter …

don't forget this:

'Your Perception Can Be Your Passport or Your Prison'

4

WHO IN THE WORLD IS AN UNDERDOG?

'Beware of barking at Underdogs; don't fight with
people who have nothing to lose'.

— Dory Previn

Have you ever felt disadvantaged? Can you recall a time when you strongly believed things were set up against you and it just wasn't a level playing ground for you? Or could it be a moment when it looked like you were surely set up to fail?

The Underdog scenario describes a David versus Goliath situation, in which a visibly smaller, less experienced, less skilled person goes head on against a bigger, more experienced, better skilled and renowned champion. By the end of this chapter, you will understand who an Underdog is and what the Underdog Mindset is all about. You will see how seemingly disadvantaged situations can flip 180° to deliver highly advantageous platforms. You will also see the Underdog inputs, and how these building blocks come together to empower you to convert setbacks to comebacks.

The term Underdog originated in the 19th century and was used for the dog that lost a dogfight. But with time, this term became an expression given to the assumed or predicted loser of a competition or contest. So basically, two things changed:

- First, a departure from the original 'dogfight' context to more general contexts.
- Next, the narrative now comes as an assumption (in the predictive sense) instead of an actual occurrence.

Have you ever felt like others expected you to fail? What were the circumstances that led to that? Would this be growing up, in school, at work, in your general relationships, or at sports? I have felt like an Underdog several times in my life where I felt I was disadvantaged, and everything was working against me.

- As a kid, I was born into a normal, happy family but, at a formative age, my parents divorced. They later restored their relationship.
- As a kid, I was abused by the helpers in my house, and I couldn't speak up.

- In the lower grades while I was at school, I struggled to keep up with other kids in sports and academically.
- When I finally got my bearing in high school, we fell into extreme financial hardship during my senior high. We were so poor, I fell ill due to malnutrition!
- I failed the university entrance exams three times in a row (yeah, yeah! I scored a hattrick of failures), and then when I managed to get into the university I couldn't afford to get basic reading materials and handouts like other students.
- On top of that, the lecturers said they knew I would be bottom of the class as I didn't appear 'serious'.
- In my MBA entrance exam, I was told I was borderline and needed to be monitored as they were not sure I could contribute effectively to the MBA program.

In life, we have many Underdog stories that inspire us. They defied all odds and created a name for themselves in the world — be it sports, business, or other fields. Let's talk about a few examples of individuals or entities who were believed to be the most unlikely to win ... people that beat the favourites nevertheless, through adversity and opposition.

Underdogs in Sports

Wilma Rudolph

Wilma didn't have such a great start. She experienced disasters from birth — being a premature baby with pneumonia, then scarlet fever, then finally, polio. The aftermath of polio left one of her legs badly crippled, with her foot twisted inward. Because of this, Wilma kept using metal braces until she got to the age of eleven.

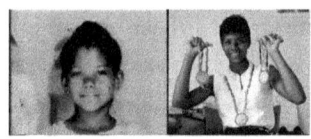

FIG 12: WILMA RUDOLPH. SOURCE: RARENEWSPAPERS.COM

Somehow, even though her situation appeared hopeless, she was replete with hope and acted accordingly. She practised walking without braces and of course, without the approval of her parents. For support, she got her sister to keep watch, just to stay safe from her parents.

Wilma continued until she had no need for her crutches! Then shortly after she started walking, she began to run. She kept practising this for a while with vigour and consistency, and, when she was sixteen Wilma won a bronze medal in a relay race at the Melbourne Olympics in Australia.

Four years later she became the first woman to secure three gold medals in track and field.

Abebe Bikila

Bikila was working as a bodyguard to the Ethiopian royal family when someone spotted his athletic potential. Still, his selection to run the marathon at the 1960 Olympic Games in Rome was a surprise to the world, since this unknown Ethiopian runner was whisked into the Olympics marathon as a replacement for a teammate.

FIG 13: ABEBE BIKILA. SOURCE: AP NEWS

When Bikila arrived in Rome, he had no shoes. He had tried running in a pair that weren't the right fit for him, but decided to do away with them and run barefoot. Who was this unknown, unprofessional green horn and what global embarassment they would bring to the Ethiopian (and by extension Sub Saharan African) race? People thought that this would be such a shameful end to the Olympics, but … as an Underdog, Bikila had nothing to lose and went on barefooted in the race!

The race continued and people watched with bated breath watching a barefooted unknown Bikila only pulling away from Rhadi — the favourite from Morocco — in the closing 500m of the race. Bikila sprinted so incredibly hard that he won by

25 seconds, breaking the world record. The Underdog of the race had won the prestigious Olympic marathon and placed Ethiopia, as well as Sub-Saharan Africa, on the list of gold winners for the first time ever! When Bikila was asked about his decision to run bare footed, he said, 'I wanted the world to know that my country, Ethiopia, has always won with determination and heroism'.

The story remains incredible — a runner who wasn't supposed to be in Rome for the Olympics, and didn't even have running shoes, ended up out-performing the favourite by atheletically huge 25-second margin.

Team Morocco

One very recent Underdog story that the world will never forget is the Moroccan national team's performance in the 2022 World Cup in Qatar. Morocco made history by becoming the first African and Arabic-speaking country to go to the semifinals in the first World Cup held in the Middle East and played in a majority-Muslim nation.

FIG 14. MOROCCO'S YAHIA ATTIYAT ALLAH WAVES HIS COUNTRY'S FLAG AS HE CELEBRATES WITH TEAMMATES AFTER THEIR 1-0 WIN OVER PORTUGAL IN A WORLD CUP QUARTERFINAL SATURDAY IN DOHA, QATAR.
(MARTIN MEISSNER / ASSOCIATED PRESS)

No one ever expected the type of soccer ability, the sheer display of resilience, and the incredible level of performance from a team that was not expected to progress through group stages! The team, in a true Underdog scenario, brought down three of the World Cup favourites — Belgium, Spain and Portugal — to gain a ticket to the semi-finals.

> 'We are the Rocky of this World Cup. When you watch 'Rocky' you want to support Rocky Balboa. Now the world is with Morocco'.
>
> — Moroccan coach Walid Regragui

In Business

As in every endeavour, we have Underdogs in the corporate world as well.

The Underdogs in business often, surprisingly, disrupt legacy strategies and markets. They re-design value chains by creating more efficient business processes as they encourage other players to think outside the square. This brings hope to aspiring employees and entrepreneurs as they prove that hard work, perseverance, optimism, and grit can initiate required change — from marginal improvements, to breakthrough improvements, and finally, disruptive improvements.

Corporate Underdogs

Netflix

Netflix started out with humble beginnings in 1997, hitting unprecedented fame by 2005, and becoming a household need during COVID-19. The financial and business success recorded by Netflix during COVID-19 remains unparalleled as the lockdowns and quarantines fuelled even greater demand. Despite Netflix being a technological powerhouse and an extremely successful company, there are still many things that the public might not know about their Underdog days. Let's delve into some little known facts about Netflix.

The company began in 1997; they innovated movie rentals by revamping Blockbuster's business model of renting DVDs and instead allowed their customers to rent DVDs by mail as well. Instead of charging per DVD rented, they adopted a flat monthly fee pricing structure for their services. Unfortunately, this resulted in the demise of chain movie rental businesses including Blockbuster and by 2005, Netflix acquired the loyalty of 4.2 million rental subscribers. Two years later, in 2007, they announced that they would expand their business model to also allow for TV and movie streaming directly to PCs. It wasn't long until Netflix was made available on other devices such as Xbox, Apple, various television models, smartphones, and tablets. This versatility and innovation to personal entertainment services has enabled Netflix to be easily accessible for households worldwide.

Apple

Apple, as most people know, is the most valuable brand on the planet, worth $2.1 trillion (December 2022), which places it ~17% ahead of both Aramco and Alphabet.

Steve Jobs invested everything into developing novel and distinctive technology in order to outdo Microsoft, the leading electronics and computing company at the time. The iPod came through as a mega disruption when it was released by Apple, completely redefining how we listened to music and seamlessly substituted the Walkman. Subsequently the iPhone and iPad changed the game in the mobile phone arena, and gradually unseated mobile phone juggernauts such as Nokia.

Ben & Jerry's

In Burlington, Vermont, two friends — Ben & Jerry's — spent $5 on an ice cream-making correspondence course and eventually built their first ice cream parlour after investing $12,000 ($8,000 from savings, and $4,000 borrowed). The industry leaders — Haagen-Dazs (the Pillsbury Company) — were aware of this and tried to pre-emptively destroy Ben & Jerry's operation. Their efforts, however, proved futile as Ben & Jerry's use of fresh local (Vermont) milk and cream, substantial chocolate chunks, and fresh fruit, was unmatchable. This was handmade ice-cream with an excellent brand strategy. Ben & Jerry's shares continued to grow and they are currently the leading ice cream brand in the United States in 2022, based on sales at $0.9Bn (Statista reports, Dec. 2022).

Scotland — The Military Underdog

Most of us have seen the movie *Braveheart*, but there were a few historical inaccuracies that need to be dispelled. Firstly, William Wallace wasn't 5ft 9inches tall, but rather reports suggest he was 8-10 inches taller; the Scotsmen didn't fight in kilts; and the battle of Stirling Bridge actually happened on a bridge.

FIG 15: WALTER BOWER 2008 (SCOTICHRONICON BKS XI-XII)

Mel Gibson had the bridge cut from the scene, claiming it was too 'Jew-y!'

So, the story goes ... England had significantly underestimated Scotland and expected to defeat them easily because they outnumbered them at a 5 to 1 ratio. The English had 8,000 to 10,000 infantry, while the Scots had 2,000, and 1,000 to 2,000 cavalry against 300 Scotsmen on horses. The Scottish arsenal was obviously less sophisticated, as they didn't have the armoury of the English. The Scotsmen were massively outnumbered, had only horses as their war vehicles, and were up against the English Longbows that were reputed to be the most feared and elite arsenal on the planet at the time! And the Scots were just brave men on horses!

The real Underdog of them all, William Wallace (described in the chronicle *Scotichronicon* as 'a tall man with the body of a giant'), knew there was no way his men could face the English cavalry on normal terms and so, embarked on an insane plan — insane but truly effective as an art of war strategy! Wallace arranged his men in a square formation to dilute the impact of the feared English Longbows, and with this, successfully forced the English into a choke point — the narrow Stirling Bridge. The idea was that since the bridge was only wide enough for two mounted units to cross at one time, it would constrain the English to a point where the battle would be 'more evenly matched' and they would have to line up and attack one or two at a time.

FIG 16: CHAPTER ILLUSTRATION

At the end, almost half of the English army was slain by the Underdog Scotsmen!

The Underdog Identity Code

There's nothing more inspiring than seeing an Underdog in any endeavour climbing up that hill in a relentless pursuit of the number one position, as they prevail through all odds and adopt the right perspective, built on a strong belief and sheer determination. These great examples give us all hope that we can get started on any endeavour — business, sports, personal goals etc. — and make that into a legacy, if only we persist.

As was said many years ago:

> *'It's not the size of the dog in the fight,
> it's the size of the fight in the dog!'*

— Mark Twain

FIG 17: CHAPTER ILLUSTRATION

Adopting the Underdog identity points an individual or a corporate organisation toward continuous improvement.

The Underdog is not the wolf at the top of the mountain; rather, the Underdog is the wolf still climbing that mountain and so his hunger is unparalleled!

Generally, the Underdog Mindset is deployed across endeavours to induce a mindset that is unstoppable.

A study conducted by the University of South Florida in 2005 shared interesting insights about how leaders can cultivate this

Underdog spirit within their organisations and empower teams with the required confidence to remain unstoppable. According to Nadav (2005, pp. 33), establishing an identity as an Underdog might provide the drive and effort required to overcome significant obstacles and succeed. As a result, Underdog stories are frequently employed by contemporary organisations, from high-tech companies to professional sports teams, to motivate employees to achieve their goals. To establish the Underdog identity within teams, the researchers insisted that the leader's credibility be established. Basically, if a leader demonstrates a track record of success, then that helps to generate that identity critical to the unstoppable mindset.

The Underdog Mentality

Success means different things to different people, but in one way or another, success connects to our ability to achieve our goals. The Underdog mentality can help us preserve that winning mindset (regardless of whether we're super successful or pushing to become successful) as it allows us to keep leveraging the Underdog winning formula regardless of our status.

A Personal Experience

I have been underrated, underestimated, under anticipated … just name it! It's music to my ears when this happens as it means the expectations are very low and so when I deliver, I over deliver. The write offs are a turn on for me; the push backs are a platform for me. I prepare so rigorously and so consistently that when showtime comes, it's usually familiar terrain for me!

I recall when I was getting into college, I had successfully failed the entrance exams so many times that my dad asked me not to bother aiming for the top schools in the country. I was to look for the less selective and competitive schools where I would stand a greater chance of entry! My dad's vote of no confidence unleashed the Underdog spirit in me. I took that as a big lifetime challenge and practised hard. It was during this time I learnt how to engage in deep focus and blank out everything around me, except for my target of focus. Today this 'skill' has been very beneficial to me in writing, research, unravelling business problems, and so on.

Now back to the story — so I essentially schooled myself and went in for the exams still aiming for the top schools in the country. I bought the application forms (back then it was all mainly hard copy forms) with some money I saved over time, and applied without my dad's knowledge.

I was so confident because I had done the work behind the scenes. I was delighted when the results came out and I was offered a place! Only then did I inform my dad, who was so surprised, confused, and delighted, all at the same time.

On the next page, you will find two exercises aimed at establishing the Underdog mindset. Furthermore, you will discover how you can operationalise this with your team by setting narratives that encourage Underdog thinking within the team.

Following this, we will review what we have learnt so far in this chapter.

Exercise I — Generating the Underdog Mentality

Here's a simple 6-point process for establishing the Underdog mentality

The 'trick' comes from what one chooses to think and believe in the moment. There are many mental tricks athletes use — here's how you can develop an often-used one, 'The Underdog Mentality'.

1. Brainstorm all inputs into the event. Separate the non-favourable from the favourable inputs. They could comprise things like:
    - Age (too old or too young)
    - Experience (again, this could swing both ways)
    - Skill set
    - Physical fitness (especially in sports)
    - Track record of achievements
    - Level of confidence
    - Networks

2. Seek to re-write the narrative of these non-favourable realities by turning each non-favourable into a favourable input. For example — on paper you may appear to be a rookie in terms of skill sets, but then again, that could be an opportunity for you to come into the game with 'fresh' eyes and to learn even faster than one who may need to unlearn a bit to get that fresh perspective. You may be a bit older on paper, but then again, you may have gathered very useful unique experiences which could add disproportionate value to the team ... the list goes on.
3. Seek to connect past experiences where you have leveraged your unique capabilities to deliver outstanding performances ... try to create relevant connections between those events and the current one.
4. The whole idea is to eliminate the unnecessary counterproductive pressures and build confidence.
5. Remember the difference between <u>confidence</u> (a collection of past positive memories) and <u>expectations</u> (future thoughts that typically cause nervousness).
6. Choose to stay in the present, focusing on ideal strategies and having fun.

Exercise II — Setting the Underdog Narrative

How Leaders Can Cultivate the Underdog Mindset for More Effective Team Results

1. **First things First: Co-create and Co-own the Vision.**
   To onboard the team into the true spirit of an Underdog, it's key that the team both co-creates and co-owns the vision to also drive more accountability and more passion. This will build collective cohesion within the team.

2. **Connect by Being More Human (disclose your mistakes, vulnerabilities etc.).**
   Unlike most approaches, we need to show the human side of us to connect in depth and breadth with our team members. By positioning yourself as an Underdog, you can capture ethical stereotypes normally attached to Underdogs and thus resonate more strongly with the team members.

3. **Run with the Speed of Trust.**
   To achieve the highest levels of performance, you need to activate unbridled trust. Trust needs to be at maximum levels to reduce bureaucratic bottlenecks and unnecessary filters. Underdogs need full trust to operate at full capacity at work.

What Did We Learn?

We started this chapter by defining the term Underdog. I shared a few personal stories about how I fully resonate with this concept and then we delved into the Underdog as a universal concept cutting across several endeavours.

We looked at Underdog stories — personal examples, sports, business, and also military — showing how, time and again, the 'disadvantaged' Underdog unseated the favourite. We then assessed the Underdog mindset from a research lens to see how objective studies correlate with what we see. Finally, we ended the chapter with clear tips for anyone to adopt the Underdog mindset and channel this into become a competitive strategy.

What's Next?

Now it's time to unpack more details of the Underdog Code. What are the main aspects of an Underdog? How does this work together to establish the Underdog Code, which then positions us to win in the game of life by introducing sustainable competitive advantages?

Stay tuned …

If you forget anything in the last chapter ...

don't forget this:

'The Underdog Turns Pain into Propane!'

5

THE UNDERDOG DOESN'T PLAY FAIR

'Being underestimated is one of the biggest
competitive advantages you can have. Embrace it!'

— Unknown

We all know how it feels when we hold a competitive advantage in something. Can you recall those few things you do much more effectively than others? It could be the way you deliver on a specific task. Maybe you have acquired so much skill that you do this almost subconsciously. Perhaps you have extraordinary endurance and you're able to endure a particular journey much better than others.

What if I told you that conversely, those things you feel you suck at would in fact endow you with even more competitive advantage than those you think you're way better at?

By the end of this chapter, you will see how your setback can be your comeback; how your disadvantages can become your superpowers, and how circumstances affecting you negatively can become the wind pushing your sail. You will understand how the Underdog mindset can position you so you have an unfair advantage over your contemporaries in all walks of life.

The David and Goliath story is one of the most famous and widely celebrated tales from the Old Testament in the Holy Bible. Everyone familiar with biblical stories is likely to know the David and Goliath story. The narrative is that David, as a young, inexperienced boy, slew the formidable giant Goliath. The story therefore comes across as a truly inspiring example of how an Underdog flipped the narrative to achieve the improbable — defeat someone much bigger than him, against all the odds.

Except, there are two queries within this story:

- First, was Goliath really positioned to win? And …
- Second, perhaps even more intriguingly: was David really the Underdog in that fight?

David and Goliath: The Popular Narrative

So, according to the popular account of David's fight with Goliath, the Philistines had challenged the Israelites to a battle and as such, the Israelites were getting ready. Each of the challengers stood on a mountain with a valley separating the two armies. Goliath, the Philistine's flag bearer, was said to be a giant of over nine feet tall, wearing his full suit of armour. He also carried a huge spear. Just picture him — the dude must have looked incredibly daunting!

Every day, Goliath would walk out and challenge the Israelite army to send a representative to engage him in a single combat. The winner of the single combat would signify the winner of the dispute between the nations. So basically, if Goliath won, then it would be a Philistine victory, but if the Israelite representative won, then the Israelites would be the victors. And of course, the winner takes all!

With Goliath's size, experience, and constant taunting; the Israelites became greatly frightened about their fate. There was national fear starting from their King, Saul, down to the most junior member of the Israelite camp. Goliath had successfully established a national crisis in Israel … in today's world, Israel may have declared a state of national emergency!

To everyone's surprise though, David, a young shepherd-boy, accepted the challenge and declared his interest to take on the

Philistine flag bearer. To the deep shock of everyone, he stepped out to face Goliath. David had the most unconventional weaponry one could imagine. His arsenal comprised:

- A bag with five smooth stones that he had picked from the nearby brook
- His sling
- His staff

Goliath started to provoke David, cursing him, and taunting him in different ways, but David replied that the Lord, *his* God, would support him in striking Goliath down and make the Israelites victorious over the Philistines. As he heard the words of David, Goliath moved to attack him. David rushed towards the battlefield and used his sling to hurl a stone at Goliath. The stone struck Goliath on his forehead and caused the Philistine giant to fall to the ground. David then stood over him and beheaded him. Immediately, the Philistines retreated and fled the battle, while David took Goliath's armour and transported the head to Jerusalem.

David and Goliath: The Real Deal — Unfair Advantages

Now, let's see the real deal. You may have considered the story of David and Goliath as the story of a weak shepherd boy defeating a mighty experienced warrior. However, to the surprise of many (myself included a while ago), the converse is truly the case!

It turns out to be quite different from what we may have envisioned. Now, without making you feel bad about holding the wrong conclusion from the beginning, I want you to know that this is the very essence of the Underdog mentality — *we never see it coming*!

There are three key areas that work as inputs to activating an Underdog's Superpower. These inputs are clearly displayed by David and show how he moved from apparent disadvantage, to the favourite, by flipping the scenario around and making Goliath the disadvantaged one!

These are:

- His Strategy (here we will refer to his military strategy)
- His Configuration (as this is a military battle, we will refer to his physical configuration)
- His Tools & Techniques (we will call this his skillset as this would be the sum total of his knowledge, ability, and experience leveraging his tools)
- His Pre-works (we will call this his rituals)

1. Military Strategy

What most would think:
Goliath was said to have been 'a warrior from his youth'. But outside of this, Goliath was the nationally acclaimed champion of the Philistines, and so we had an experienced giant who knew nothing else but how to win on the battle ground. To add more wind to his sail, he had the full support and backing of his entire nation. Talk about a well-established legacy and support system ... but there's a bit more to this!

What the reality was:
In ancient warfare, every army would comprise any or a hybrid of these three different types of warriors:

- The cavalry
- The heavy infantry
- The artillery

The heavy infantry are the foot soldiers, usually armed with swords and shields and similar weaponry. The cavalry are men on horsebacks and those who ride with chariots. Finally, we have the artillery that is comprised of archers and slingers.

David's strategy was completely disruptive at the time. He took advantage of his opponent's resources and capabilities and designed a fool-proof game changing strategy! David's strength in artillery — specifically as an experienced slinger— was clearly

Goliath's weakness as Goliath knew nothing more than the heavy infantry way of engaging in battle. This meant Goliath would be crippled by any method which defied physical contact. On the contrary, the aerial warfare methods were David's forte!

Most of the time, when we refer to 'strategy', we are likely to be talking strategy in business. However, the best strategies in business originated from warfare tactics. Sun Tsu — one of the greatest military strategists of all time — influences many business strategists. They're summed in his legacy book *The Art of War*.

A few of the key principles shared by Sun Tsu in *The Art of War* can be seen in David and Goliath, such as:

- *All warfare is based on deception. Hence, when able to attack we must seem unable. When using our forces, we must seem inactive. When we are near, we make the enemy believe we are far away. When far away we must make the enemy believe we are near.*
- *Appear weak when you are strong, and strong when you are weak.*
- *If he is superior in strength, evade him.*
- *Attack him where he is unprepared. Appear where you are not expected.*

These principles were fully adopted and adapted by our inexperienced Israelite champion — Master David.

2. Physical Configuration

What most would think:
Goliath was from the lineage of Gath, known to be home to a number of giants and so it wasn't such a surprise that Goliath was a giant — a mighty, 6-foot-9 Philistine warrior. So here we are with a mighty dude by all standards — whether in today's world or in ancient times. Such a giant could crush anyone in seconds, right? Well ... not so fast. Let's see why!

What the reality was:
Scientists have proven that at that height and configuration, Goliath was likely to have had a medical disorder known as *acromegaly*. This condition induces two significant traits: extreme physical growth acceleration and extreme double-vision and near-sightedness. So basically, Goliath was unable to see clearly at 'moderate distances' as he suffered severe near-sightedness and was nearly blind! This may also explain why he had to be 'escorted' to the battlefield.

3. Skillset

What most would think:
The popular belief is that David came into battle with just a sling whilst Goliath was outfitted to crush him. Goliath's full armour would protect him and at the same time afford him the resources to annihilate David at first attack!

Again, the tables turned to the surprise of everyone!

What the reality was:

David initially intended to go into conventional battle with Goliath, as we're told that, on Saul's direction, he set out to put on a coat of armour and a brass helmet and he girded himself with a sword. But then he retraced his steps and carefully informed King Saul, '*I cannot go in these, because I am not used to them*' (New International Version Bible, (1973) — 1st Samuel 17:39). So, he took them off.

He then went back to the tools he was used to, which include his staff, his sling, and his five smooth stones from the stream that he put into the pouch of his shepherd's bag.

Altogether, these seemingly 'basic' tools actually were a *highly destructive mechanism*! David's deadly ammunition comprised his leather pouch with two long cords attached to it, and his five selected stones or rocks. Thus, David's sling was an undeniably devastating weapon and, what made things even worse was that this was not common knowledge. So, Goliath was likely to be unaware of what he was coming up against.

Again, remember Sun Tsu's guidance:

- *All warfare is based on deception.*
- *Attack him where he is unprepared. Appear where you are not expected.*

When David whirled around the sling, he was doing so at around 6-7 revolutions per second. That's incredible momentum!

Malcom Gladwell provides a deep insight into this competitive advantage held by David. According to Gladwell, the stone that came out from his sling was as fast as a bullet from a .45mm handgun. So, when it hit the giant's forehead it was as fatal as a gunshot. The 'rocks' found in the valley of Elah are not normal rocks. They are made of barium sulphate, twice the density of normal stones.

So, David walks right up to Goliath (but still far enough away that Goliath's swords and javelin are useless) and kills him with a single shot to the head. Slingers, as historical records show, were incredibly accurate, even capable of hitting birds in flight. Most probably, this would be like our modern-day Darrell Pace of the US or even more recently global champions like Park Sung-Hyun, who is arguably one of the greatest Olympic archers of the 21st century!

So, David leveraged his competitive advantage being a connoisseur in aerial battle where he completely rendered the heavy infantry champion irrelevant! The three points being: his military *strategy*; his physical *configuration*, and his skillset, driven by his *tools and techniques*, came together as David's organised arsenal of competitive advantages against Goliath.

4. Rituals

What most would think:
There is, however, one more thing that is obscured — the unknown track record of training David had undergone for many years. The general understanding would have been that David didn't have that military track record that Goliath had, and he basically just had experience tending his flock, right?

As usual, Underdogs always pop up when least expected!

What the reality was:
David had a great deal of experience attacking 'giants' (lions and bears) that came for his flock. These very powerful, dexterous, and extremely skilled contenders were habitually defeated by David as part of his rituals ... his daily activity system. This meant that, as far as David was concerned, he was very much at home with engaging in battle with giants and it was part of his daily beat!

> 'But David said to Saul, "Your servant used to keep his father's sheep, and when a lion or a bear came and took a lamb out of the flock, I went out after it and struck it, and delivered the lamb from its mouth; and when it arose against me, I caught it by its beard, and struck and killed it. Your servant has killed both lion and bear; and this uncircumcised Philistine will be like one of them, seeing he has defied the armies of the living God'" (1 Samuel 17:34-36).

So basically, David had an excellent performance record, and his preparation and diligence in the background built the right confidence and skill set he needed to take on Goliath in the battle.

The story of David defeating Goliath will forever remain a powerful tale. The message it imparts to all individuals across the globe is invaluable. It reveals to us how David demonstrated the unstoppable quality of a true Underdog, showing a keen ability to leveraging military strategies to defeat a much larger favourite.

The Favourites Are Expected to Win

One of the biggest reasons why Underdogs enjoy an unfair advantage is because they are expected to lose! Yes, yes … that may not sound super intelligible, but this is exactly the point. We're used to seeing 'successful' as the favourite, correct? That super smart girl in class who may not even know what it means, let alone what it feels like, to fail a course; or that dude in the bank who just keeps smashing all the targets and dwarfs the performance of others during the weekly reviews.

You know what's common about these exceptional people? They're pace setters; they're standard bearers. Sometimes, they're used as yardsticks for assessing the performance of others within the team. But then again, they're under a lot of pressure. They just *must* deliver! It's now part of their DNA and failure isn't even an option.

Counterintuitively, this can be positive for the Underdog. Remember, no one even acknowledges the Underdog because he's expected to lose! He's not known to win … that's certainly not part of his DNA, at least from the viewpoint of the experts!

As individuals, we can sometimes get to a point where the challenge is not as strong as before and therefore, we get complacent or content with things the way they are. This is one of the major challenges favourites face. The hunger becomes diluted and affects the motivation to win. The opposite is the case for the Underdogs. They are extremely hungry and desperate to win, and so they're far from complacent. They don't understsnd what complacency even means!

A Personal Experience

When I first came into academia as a rookie, my teaching was expected to be just average, or maybe even low, as I had no classroom teaching experience. These low expectations were all I needed to shine. My strategy was to raise the bar significantly, by combining the expected teaching standards with my expertise as an industry experienced, commercial c-suite executive, and author in motivation/self-help spaces. My configuration was my industry experience that was beneficial to my students as they saw a firsthand connection between theory and practice.

My skillset comprised several engaging tools I would use during my capability trainings in my previous commercial roles, the tools I would use to ensure a seamless presentation based on my consultancy works. These ensured my classes were full of excitement and I could de-mystify complex business problems with easy to grasp solutions. My rituals came through as a certain collection of practices that ensured I always performed at my peak, regardless of the situation. And so, I constantly exceeded all expectations!

What Did We Learn?

The chapter started by providing a unique insight into the dearly loved story of the number one Underdog in history — David as he battled Goliath. The story helped us understand how the Underdog operates, leveraging the art of war. We were able to understand that the Underdog mindset is key to positioning our thinking and actions, which ultimately turn our seemingly unfair advantages into our key ammunition, guaranteeing that we emerge victorious.

Next Steps

The next page summarises the unfair advantage Underdogs hold over the so called favourites. In similar fashion to the David & Goliath story, we have three principles that guarantee an Underdog is able to flip the disadvantages to serve his superpower. Then we have one key ingredient to make this sustainable — practice! This is our 3+1 formula card that results in the incredible advantage an Underdog possesses. When put together, this formular card unleashes the Underdog's Superpower:

1. Strategy
2. Configuration (mental, physical etc)
3. Skillset via tools & techniques
   +
1. Iterate via practice to establish rituals

The 3+1 Underdog Formula Card

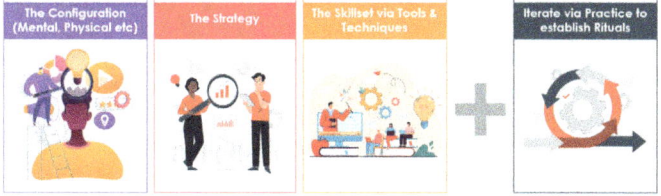

FIG 18: CHAPTER ILLUSTRATION

Exercise I

Now you are required to do four things:

1. Pick an example from the past where you considered yourself an Underdog and assumed you had disadvantages that excluded you from being the favourites.

2. Now that you know the Underdog's advantages can flip 180 degrees to be their superpowers, you need to show what you would do differently in the scenario you noted above.
3. Simulate the outcome of the event based on your revised perspective and your refocused activity system.
4. Run a simple comparison placing what you would make happen (by leveraging the Underdog mindset) against what actually did happen in the past.

If you forget anything in the last chapter ...

don't forget this:

'The Underdog Converts Failures into Fuel!'

6

THE UNDERDOG PIVOTS

'Pivoting isn't plan B: it's part of the process'.

— Jeff Goins

Think about it. If you tried to plot a line that reflects the pathway taken by any successful person (success here being subjective) would it be straight? Or would it have some detours … some pivots … some inflections, etc.? Chances are it won't be a straight plot! In most cases either you decide to take a detour in your life, or life itself serves you some very interesting curveballs! So, the ability to adapt to different situations remains one of the most critical skills we can sharpen as individuals. If one is resolute and rigid in their ways, they most likely won't be able to handle change and this will almost guarantee that happiness or meaningful purpose become elusive. It's critical to pay attention to today's trends, predict the future, and have a keen awareness of your skillsets.

By the end of this chapter, you will understand how the power to pivot is one of the most compelling tools used by Underdogs. You will see how Underdogs pivot in a hybrid display of agility, adaptability, and remarkable velocity and how they can fail forward in situations that normally would crush others. This skill enables them to become better versions of themselves on a day-to-day basis.

The Power to Pivot

Just imagine what would've transpired if Arnold Schwarzenegger hadn't made the pivots in his career. He could've stopped when he was the world champion bodybuilder in his 20s, and continued to walk that path to perhaps become a coach. Odds are we may not have felt his significance as we feel it today. His contribution and value creation in the world today may have not become evident. Thankfully, he pivoted and embraced Hollywood to become an award-winning actor in his 30s and then, just when we thought Arnold had found his dream and would remain there, he decided to pivot again to become the Governor of California in 2003 at 56.

One of the best untold and unfair advantages an Underdog has is the power to pivot. Just think about it! Underdogs are able to make mistakes, learn from those mistakes, and use those learnings to continuously improve on their overall approach.

Why is this the case? It's simply because Underdogs have the mindset of improving continuously. They love to learn and hold the same level of curiosity that little kids have. You must have heard at some point how a typical 4-year-old asks a million 'whys' about everything! They do this out of curiosity, which can increase during that part of their learning and development. In the same way, the Underdog is as humble as a kid and is ready to listen, learn, and re-apply learnings to continuously improve. Like the 4-year-olds, the Underdogs are not afraid to make mistakes. Here though, the way that Underdogs make mistakes needs to be observed; they make their mistakes quickly and on small scales. Basically, they fail forward and pivot fast.

Most of my close friends know I love foosball. It's really relaxing for me, whether I play alone or with others. I developed my love for foosball during the lockdown when COVID-19 hit in 2020.

For those unfamiliar with the game, its simply soccer played on a table that resembles a mini pool (snooker) table. Foosball is a very fast-paced game where at any time two teams alternate between offensive play (i.e., when a team has the ball and is actively attempting to score a goal) and defensive play (i.e., when a team is actively attempting to stop the opposing team from scoring a goal).

Foosball players frequently need to pivot, which, in this context, refers to physically being able to go from one direction, pause, then go in another direction in a very short amount of time. In fact, the game of foosball is replete with the need to constantly pivot. This forces the player to change hands while in the process of converting from defence to offence, and vice versa. Knowing how to use this tactic effectively can be the difference between making a play to score the winning goal, and missing a play to stop the goal that seals the win for the opposing team.

We all experience occasions in life where we can and/or should pivot, just like you would do in foosball. We face occasions where we need to take a detour. Pivots are necessary in both professional and commercial settings, as well as in everyday life. Knowing when and how to pivot improves our ability to shift course when necessary and increases the likelihood that we will succeed in achieving our objectives.

What Does It Mean to Pivot?

Here I would like us to consider the word pivot as a verb and explore what the Merriam-Webster dictionary has to say about it (the second meaning of the verb Pivot): *to adapt or improve by adjusting or modifying something (such as a product, service, or strategy)*. Essentially, pivoting means to change directions.

Some of us may have seen the very popular sitcom 'Friends'. There was one interesting episode where Ross was trying to move a sofa up the stairs of an NYC walk-up alongside Joey and Rachel. The unforgettable part in the scene was when Ross kept screaming '*Pivhhhaaaattt*' without giving any instruction about how, or even why, it should work. Don't blame him. Pivoting can be much more complex and may even present broader implications. The act of pivoting itself can be likened to a phrase in *Agile Project Management* known as 'progressive elaboration'.

The technique of continuously refining requirements as a project develops is known as progressive elaboration and is predominantly used in Project Management, when managing projects in an 'Agile' environment. This may sound a bit counterintuitive as one would expect to have all plans clearly defined very early in the project; but actually, the converse is true as this process can lead to better optimisation of resources, where estimates become sharper and more accurate as the project progresses towards its completion.

'Pivoting is our way of Adapting'.

We have been taught in biology, or watched in National Geographic videos, or seen in real life, how plants and animals are able to adapt. You may have heard of a lizard regrowing its tail after losing the original tail to a hawk or a cat; camels have long eyelashes (and a third eyelid) to keep sand out of their eyes and a huge signature hump, which is full of fat that they can metabolise when there is no food or water around; chameleons change colour in order to camouflage according to the surroundings and also as a part of their mating process. Plants, like cactus that grow in the desert, have adapted the structure of their roots to be able to thrive with very little rainfall. Some plants have adapted to take advantage of any rainfall that occurs while others have adapted to look for water very deep in the ground.

But all these are incomparable to the level of adaptability humans possess. We are designed to adapt, and pivoting is the vehicle that brings this to life in humans. We adapt by learning and pivot by implementing. Hence, we're able to pivot to do anything we want to do. We just need to learn how.

> 'To improve is to change;
> to be perfect is to change often'.
>
> — Winston Churchill

A Few Remarkable Pivots in History

1. YouTube

Even though it's difficult to picture, YouTube as anything other than the wildly popular video streaming service it is now, its early years weren't quite as popular. When it was first launched, it was intended to be a sort of video-based dating site where users could upload brief videos outlining their perfect mate and search for matches. The website's tagline was 'Tune in, hook up'.

YouTube then pivoted quickly into the empire that Google purchased for $65bn when it foresaw the future based on YouTube's enormous potential.

2. Walt Disney

If feels impossible to think that the one who defined 'imagination' with the most innovative offerings within the world of visual arts — mimicking reality — which we now call 'animations', was once said to 'lack imagination'!

As ridiculous as it sounds, it's the truth! Walt Disney, who was previously a newspaper editor, was fired because 'he lacked imagination and had no good ideas'. Well, look at Disney today!

3. Wrigley

William Wrigley Jr. didn't always sell gum. As a matter of fact, he discovered the worth of gum by giving it away for free. In the 1890s, Mr. Wrigley Jr. relocated to Chicago and began working as a salesman of soap and baking soda. Chewing gum turned out to be more popular than his actual product once he got the notion to give it away with purchases. Years later, Wrigley started making his own brands of chewing gum, including Juicy Fruit, Spearmint, and finally, Double Mint. Today, Wrigley is a household name!

4. Instagram

One of the most popular iPhone and Android photo apps is Instagram, although not everyone is familiar with its history. Burbn, a check-in application with Mafia Wars inspired gaming and a photo component, was Instagram's predecessor. The founders feared Burbn would never catch on because of its excess clutter and potential activities; to simplify, they eliminated most of the functionality elements save for photographs. The program was completely rebuilt with a photography-only focus; it was neat and uncomplicated, and, as we know today, that was an excellent pivot!

Pivoting: What to Note

We need to be pro-active in changing the course of action once we see our plans or strategies can no longer serve us. We must learn to retrace our footsteps, get back to the drawing board and refire. While we do this, we must remember:

- Humility will be invaluable, especially at the start of pivoting, as a willingness to acknowledge our errors is key.
- Pivoting does not mean starting from ground zero. You will most likely leverage your legacy knowledge while doing so.
- Knowledge in the form of relevant information would be the foundation for a successful pivot.

The good news is that we can get better at pivoting as we gain experience. We're able to draw relevant connections every time we go through an event or suffer a consequence in life, and these connections help us re-evaluate our decisions. Every experience builds a memory bank in our brains that we can access whenever we get the impulse to take an action on our current pathway. The more we allow this learning, the better we become — to the point where we're able to anticipate changes far in advance, in the same way a master chess player does when she foresees 20 moves or more.

A Personal Experience

Pivoting is essential, it's one of the ways we learn and grow as humans. I have had to make quite a few pivots in my journey and what I have found out is that each time I pivot it appears to be that I'm multiplying my capabilities. This is because when I make the connections between the previous and the current based on the new pivot, I discover points of leverage.

You will always have experience that can be reapplied as you pivot, and this can give you a head start. A few pivots I have made have helped me see that there is no wasted knowledge, except if it's unused!

At one point in my career, I pivoted from core commercial management into academia. This was a sharp pivot, but it was an excellent move for me as I could re-apply lots of capabilities. Furthermore, the new capabilities I acquired in research, coupled with my commercial capabilities, formed me into a global consultant on commercial and C-suite projects.

This is how 1+1 became 11 for me!

What Did We Learn?

In this chapter, we saw that the ability to pivot is one of the Underdog's unique advantages, as this ensures she continually improves. We saw how many successful individuals, businesses, and other endeavours, adopted pivots to position them on the right path for greatness. We also learnt that pivoting doesn't mean starting from ground zero — nothing we have experienced or learnt will ever go to waste if we channel it appropriately. If anything, pivoting enables us to consolidate our legacies into one holistic strategy to win!

Next Steps

The next page walks us through a particular endeavour you're currently engaged with (pick three or less, to keep it simple), and considers where you would like to get to, and how you can execute the 'pivot' in a simple effective way.

THE UNDERDOG PIVOTS 99

Pivots are necessary indicators of the need for us to embrace change

Identify your current position in your career, relationship, health etc. and transparently write down three things lacking:

1) ------------
2) ------------
3) ------------

Identify what you're missing from your current status. List out the three key things that once activated would get you closer to your ideal state:

1) ------------
2) ------------
3) ------------

The hardest part is usually the first step. Let's make it a bit easier. List out the top three simple things you can do to get started on your pivots:

1) ------------
2) ------------
3) ------------

FIG 19: CHAPTER ILLUSTRATION

If you forget anything in the last chapter …

don't forget this:

'The Underdog Holds the Power to Pivot!'

7

THE UNDERDOG HAS THE 'NOT YET' MINDSET

'No doesn't mean never, it just means not yet …'

— Candice Accola

Have you ever noticed how some people appear excited almost every time you see them, while others require a push to get them on the same frequency? The common word that would serve as an answer to this is 'motivation'. The question then is why are some more motivated than others? Why do some of us seem like we've reached our end game when we get to a particular point, whereas for others, it looks like the game has just started and they're extremely hopeful even to the end?

In this section of the book, you will understand how motivation gets built up and sustained; and you will see how the Underdog perceives '*no*' as the '***next opportunity***'. This becomes the 'not yet' mindset, which is the foundation that makes the Underdog truly unstoppable.

Motivation

Science has found that the source of motivation comes from the part of the brain known as the *nucleus accumbens*. It's in the small section where neurotransmitters send chemical messages to the rest of your body. It's these neurotransmitters that keep us alert and focused. It's this part of the brain that influences things like completing a project or going to the gym.

The DOSE

The brain chemicals known as DOSE — Dopamine, Oxytocin, Serotonin, and Endorphin — are referred to as 'happy hormones' or your 'success hormones' because, in addition to elevating your mood, they also furnish you with optimism, energy, the ability to connect with others, and the capacity to unlock greater focus. All of these improve your drive, leadership, and self-assurance at work. Although you may not have been able to control all aspects of your workplace — like the people, pre-established rules etc. — you will still be able to take the necessary steps required to activate the proper hormones and be aware of every scenario you encounter! How? Let's go further to unlock this!

1. Dopamine — The Dope That Means You Can Achieve Your Goals!

Dopamine is a hormone and neurotransmitter that is a crucial component of your brain's reward system and is also referred to as the 'feel-good' hormone. Dopamine is linked to, amongst other things: learning, memory, and motor functions. It is your success hormone. Your body's dopamine levels determine how alert, focused, and creative you are. It also forms an integral part of your concentration levels and ultimately supports your long-term memory. Dopamine is the hormone that makes you want to work hard to achieve goals because of the reward you will receive. Higher dopamine levels are linked with greater ease at being more sociable, which clearly supports one's goal-seeking behaviour. This means one's boldness in social and professional circumstances will rise, thanks to dopamine, which is also associated with a greater socioeconomic position and a higher perception of social support. You must identify the incentives that inspire you and connect them to your goals if you want your body to produce more healthy dopamine levels at work.

The process of encouraging the release of dopamine is simple. Let's say you have a presentation to deliver to your executive board — one where you will be proposing a solution to a problem and seeking their alignment to execute your initiative.

Obviously, you may need to conduct lots of pre-work ahead of even starting your slides, to properly gather insights to the real pain and how your solution would address it effectively. In this case, as with most cases, the steepest uphill task is starting! This is because while starting, you will need to overcome the inertia that is working against your willingness to commence the project.

The good news is once you start the very first slide, you overcome that inertia and dopamine is released because of the milestone you have been able to reach. Interestingly, this then unlocks even more effort as your reward seeking buttons are now turned on (fuelled by the dopamine rush you got from hitting the last milestone). Then you gather momentum, and this is how dopamine can get you to keep progressing; because achieving the subsequent incremental milestones requires less willpower each time, so you seem to achieve your next milestones more easily, thanks to your dopamine rush.

2. Oxytocin — The Oxygen for Loyalty & Trust

Oxytocin is also known as the 'love hormone'. Oxytocin levels typically rise with physical affection like kissing, snuggling, and sex, and this hormone can also aid in promoting trust, empathy, and bonding in relationships. It could also be crucial for pregnancy, lactation, and healthy parent-child relationships. Increased levels of oxytocin will help improve workplace loyalty, trust, empathy, and generosity. These soft skills help make a holistic leader. In addition to fostering interpersonal bonding, oxytocin lowers stress and increases feelings of security and contentment. When we dedicate more time at work to encouraging, mentoring, or complimenting others, we simultaneously improve our oxytocin levels.

A brief rush of oxytocin can be brought on by just one minute of constructive social engagement. Similarly, oxytocin levels are boosted by unrestricted expression of work-appropriate emotions, including laughing aloud at a joke, welcoming others with a smile, and exchanging stories. Pay close attention when speaking with a co-worker —greater trust and productivity at work result from an increase in oxytocin in both parties. Fortunately, more face-to-face time with someone has the same effect. So, spending time with, and working with, your team really helps to combat the negative effects of working alone. Finally, oxytocin enables you to ask, 'How can I help you?' without anticipating anything in return, which creates a network of individuals who support each other.

3. Serotonin — Soar as a Leader with Serotonin

Your mood, as well as your sleep, appetite, digestion, learning capacity, and memory, are all regulated by **serotonin** and neurotransmitters. Serotonin is your leadership hormone. It increases determination, self-worth, inner fulfillment, confidence, and a sense of direction, while fighting cortisol, your stress hormone. When you display self-confidence and high levels of self-esteem and show you're able to manage stress, people feel positively towards you and want to follow your lead.

Expressing gratitude is a great boost for your serotonin levels. Try practising very small and easy tasks like complimenting people for their good work, saying hello to your colleague or even a stranger you see feeling down and depressed, sending an email to your colleague, or thanking them in person for their assistance with a project. You will be amazed at how this makes you feel; it helps you connect what you're doing to a greater cause, ultimately sustaining your serotonin levels and strengthening your leadership capacity.

4. Endorse Your Determination with Endorphins

Your body creates **endorphins** as a natural painkiller in reaction to stress or discomfort. When you interact, endorphin levels also frequently rise in response to activities that 'incentivise', like working out, having sex, or even eating. Your endorphins improve your mood and cognitive ability while easing physical discomfort and mental stress. To instantly release endorphins, choose to laugh frequently. The same is true for your neighbour, who is boosting their endorphin levels while using their laptop and headphones to listen to music. During a break, take a walk outside with a co-worker to increase endorphin levels through exercise, good company, and sunlight. Finally, try this mini-exercise to release endorphins and adrenaline: tighten your muscles while taking quick, deep breaths.

Ways to Increase Your DOSE

There are a few things we can do to up our DOSE levels and have all our hormones working together to enhance our performance.

Improve Your Pulse

Enjoy a weekly fitness routine for yourself. Select a team sport, or any other activity that appeals to you, such as jogging, cycling, swimming, dancing, or yoga. Include it in your lifestyle to reap the benefits of dopamine and endorphins while lowering the stress hormone cortisol. If that isn't an option, decide to walk a portion of the distance on your way home from work.

Alongside improving your pulse, taking deliberate deep breaths can also elevate serotonin levels and reduce stress if you are agitated and breathing rapidly. Improve your breathing rate to increase endorphin production if you lack energy.

Connect with Your Connections

Your interactions outside of work should take up most of your time. Whether it's family or friends, try to strengthen your relationships and discover a reliable supply of oxytocin and serotonin to support your success at work. Together with your family, go on that vacation, play with your niece, hang out with pals, or even walk the dog.

Draw Insights

Find a meditation practise that works for you despite how monotonous it may sound. You may reduce your stress hormones while increasing your serotonin and oxytocin levels by doing anything from sitting still and paying attention to your breath, to chanting, or even practising playing an instrument with complete focus.

Consider Your Food

Know what you're eating because it affects your hormones. To release dopamine and serotonin, consume dark chocolate. Caffeine gives you a dopamine boost, just like spicy peppers produce endorphins. To alter your mood, alter your diet.

Now that we have found out how to leverage our hormones it's time to see how we can combine this with a fundamental change in our way of thinking ... The *Not Yet Mindset!*

The Not Yet Mindset: Where Momentum Lives

$$No = Ny$$
Where No = Next Opportunity and Ny = Not Yet

THE UNDERDOG HAS THE 'NOT YET' MINDSET

FIG 20: CHAPTER ILLUSTRATION

The traffic lights, invented in 1923 by Garrett Morgan (one of the pioneer African American inventors of his time) completely revolutionised traffic control. They have three popular colours: Red, Green, and Amber. Each coloured light connotes different commands when we're at a traffic junction. 'Red' tells us to halt, 'green' signals we're ok to move, and 'amber' advises us to prepare for the next event — either stop (red) or move (green). The traffic light system has become a necessity on our roads, but it is now used for more than just for traffic control- such as ranking, grading, or appraisal templates. As expected, often, people push to get into a green and avoid a red, and amber is overlooked. However, amber depicts a transition phase as it speaks to momentum ... being in a mental disposition that places us in a 'Not Yet' mindset. This simply means, we may not be exactly where we want to be, but we've made a move in the right direction and so progressing past red, toward green.

But how does observing the assessment on an opportunity through the amber filter change things altogether or suddenly lead to that winning mindset?

FIG 21: CHAPTER ILLUSTRATION

Renowned Stanford Professor Carol Dweck has answers to questions on the 'Not Yet' state of mind. She explains in her book 'Mindset: The New Psychology of Success', how students at a Chicago high school were given the grade of 'Not Yet' if they hadn't passed all the necessary courses they needed to graduate. This was an unconventional approach to better considering tough experiences at high school, like difficulty, challenge, and failure. With the 'Not Yet' mentality, it felt a lot less final and, more importantly, indicated some light at the end of the tunnel. It suggested that change was indeed possible and there was room for improvement and time to grow into what was necessary to succeed. As Dweck explains, when you get a grade of 'Not Yet', you understand that you're on a learning curve. It offers you a path into the future. It gives you something to work towards, and to strive for. It gives you purpose. But even more than that, it makes whatever you are trying to achieve seem possible. 'Not Yet' suggests that you can and will get there, at some point; you're just not there 'yet'.

Mindsets: Growth & Fixed

Dweck talked about the fixed mindset being the understanding that talents and intelligence are fixed traits established at birth and unchangeable. A growth mindset believes that talents, skills, and intelligence are malleable traits that can and will change with disciplined practise and efforts. This fundamentally different philosophy is articulated by the appending word — yet.

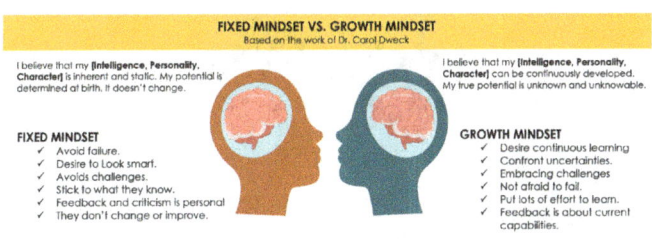

FIG 22: CHAPTER ILLUSTRATION: YAN HE, J., (2020):
PRO-GROWTH MINDSET — WHY IT'S SO IMPORTANT FOR SUCCESS.

Globally, there's been a lot of discussion on changing one's mindset and thus one's life! At face value, it does appear quite easy. Yet, when it comes to putting this into action, for instance, you will hear people talk about it being too late to learn something brand new or switch careers or even start a new life altogether and let go completely of the past. Living with these limiting beliefs can result in a self-fulfilling prophecy: if you believe you can't, then you don't. Conversely, if we live in a state of 'Not Yet', then even if we haven't achieved that goal or objective, we have a clear path to achieving it — it's just a matter of time!

I believe our thoughts have incredible power over our everyday lives, and that our moods and behaviours reflect how we think. Over the years, I've developed mental hacks to ensure I'm always in the right frame of mind to be successful and happy — and it starts with imagining possibilities instead of focusing on roadblocks.

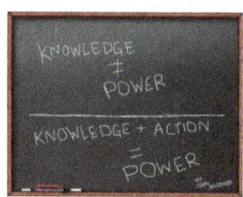

FIG 23: CHAPTER ILLUSTRATION

'Knowledge is power: You hear it all the time, but knowledge is not power. It's only potential power. It only becomes power when we apply it and use it. … If knowing is half the battle, action is the second half of the battle'.

— Jim Kwik

Bringing the Not Yet Mentality to Life

Angela Duckworth, in her book 'Grit', lays down similar principles to those of Carol Dweck. Both point to the same thing: the growth mindset, which would give rise to the 'Not Yet' mentality, is more of a practise than just a belief system that you adopt. A few areas that can help support us while activating and achieving the best out of the 'Not Yet' mindset would include:

- **Constant Reviews:** We need to continuously appraise our actions and taking stock of our activities to ensure we're truly deploying the 'Not Yet' state of mind.
- **Become the observer of our thoughts:** Stepping aside for a bit to objectively audit our thoughts. This helps to control our thoughts from drifting into the fixed mindset.
- **Embrace reality:** The reality is we will all swing between fixed and growth mindsets by default. The onus, therefore, rests on us to continuously stay on guard to swing towards the growth mindset. Bringing ourselves to terms with this is critical and ensures we can pivot back to the 'Not Yet' state of mind (growth mindset) whenever we find ourselves swaying to the fixed mindset.
- **Fail Forward:** Approaching every single failure as a learning curve will ensure we continue to 'fail forward'. This also means turning every failure into a 'lesson-learned' portfolio where we can extract the major lessons learned to re-apply in future activities.

The 'Not Yet' mentality creates a positive trajectory for continuous improvements in our daily lives, and is a proven system to drive sequential improvements in our day-to-day endeavours.

The *Not Yet Mindset* Enables the Underdog to Stay *X-traordinary*

'X'Factor: X-traordinary Habits

FIG 24: CHAPTER ILLUSTRATION

'The difference between ordinary and extraordinary is that little extra'.

— Jimmy Johnson

Do people we call 'extraordinary' do things notably differently to what 'ordinary' people do? They're willing to go a few steps beyond the rest of the crowd and, turn around ordinary levels of effort, persistence, and passion into extraordinary levels to generate ***X-traordinary*** results.

For example, the difference in scores between an A grade and a B grade could be as little as 1% point (69 vs 70) or at most, 10% points (60 vs 70). When we check to see what led to this difference, it could be as trivial as assignments completed as expected, or class attendance, or more hours put into studying. It's the little extra push that the 'A' students make that differentiates them from the 'B' students.

We're Born X-traordinary

According to Dr. Sukhi Muker, renowned wellness doctor, author, and global speaker, the first structure that developed in our mother's womb was the human nervous system comprising the brain, spinal cord, peripheral nerves, and an array of neurotransmitters. Dr. Sukhi states that the intelligence within our nervous system takes us from one cell to one trillion cells even before we're born. When you then combine this with the fact that each of those cells eventually engages in a hundred thousand chemical reactions per second (as reported by Fritz

118 THE UNDERDOG CODE

Albert Popp — leading biophysicist), then you get nothing but pure awesomeness!

This is so deep, so profound, and so mind boggling. This for me is not ordinary, this is *X-traordinary*. Even from birth, we're already designed to be *X-traordinary humans*! The only thing is how fast and well we can unleash the X-tra in the ordinary to become truly *X-traordinary*!

There are a few things we can do to realistically deploy and engage the X Habits on a daily basis that will enable us to turn the ordinary into the *X-traordinary*. We call these things the 'X-Factor'.

1. ***X-ceed*** basic routine cycles: Leverage Kata

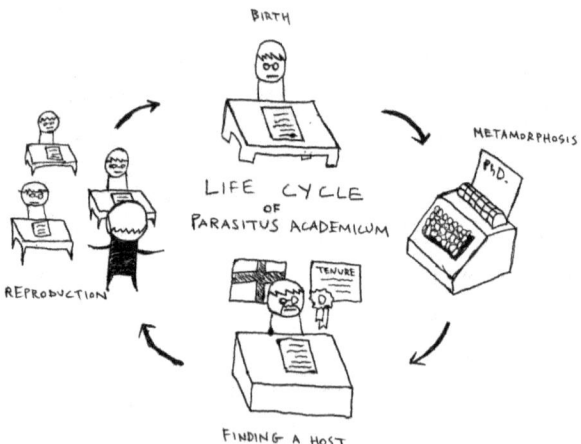

Kata is a martial art that involves deliberate, repetitive practices to master through choreographed patterns of movement that are practised until mastery of a single form is achieved.

The practice is applied again and again to learn and eventually master each small set of movements. In application, Kata is basically a form, routine, or pattern of behaviour that can be practised to develop a skill to the point where it becomes second nature.

To apply this, we need to first focus on our optimum weekly routine, deliberately implementing each element in the right frequency (daily or weekly as the case may be). With this, we not only ensure the culture and habit is second nature, we also develop ways that we can reflect on our routine and continuously improve it. When this happens, we deliberately form a habit. Forming a habit develops new skills. With new skills comes increased confidence in our abilities to recognise and make small improvements that keep a person (or a process) in top form continuously.

So, a Kata is a small but well-structured protocol or routine that becomes second nature through practice, and brings about the development of a particular skill. The point of the Kata is not the memorisation of the routines, but rather the habits of thought and action that practising them leaves behind. In other words, when we deploy the Kata approach, we set ourselves to becoming ***X-traordinary*** through the means of acquisition of new cognitive and behavioural skills, such as process improvement. Furthermore, a Kata makes these skills transferable to others — an essential part of developing a sustained culture of continuous improvement within an organisation.

2. ***X-amine*** more deeply: Unwrap your childhood curiosity

According to Harvard Business School Professor Hirotaka Takeuchi, 'A lot of times, we see things in binary terms'. But in reality, this should not be the case. We need to ask ourselves the childlike kind of questions! Just recall the way a child asks 'why' so much to satisfy their curiosity? For instance, why don't we preference 'and' instead of 'or' sometimes, or consider 'both' instead of 'either' in other cases. Allowing ourselves to be curious like little children will help us truly unlock these pertinent questions and seek to answer them accordingly — inching closer to being ***X-traordinary***.

3. ***X-plore*** more keenly: Never stop learning, never stop yearning

Comprehensive writing systems appear to have been invented centuries ago — first in Mesopotamia (present-day Iraq) where cuneiform was used between 3400 and 3300 BC, and shortly afterwards in Egypt at around 3200 BC. So, we have been in the business of information processing for quite a while! For me, one of the greatest innovations humans have been able to unlock is the ability to transmit knowledge that transcends the barrier of time. Today we have at our disposal knowledge dating back centuries, as well as cutting-edge information. The best teacher gains experience not just from their mistakes, but also the mistakes of others' — why go through the same pain another went through when you can already learn from them.

4. *X-press* your humanity: Love unconditionally

Tony Robbins perfectly summarised that 'the secret to living is giving'. This phrase has resonated with me for a long time and was further clarified by Dr. Wayne Dyer when he explained how serotonin is released in the brain when we give to others.

Giving to others brings manifold positive effects in social groups and directly helps us to feel good. We feel even better when others feel good too. In this way, giving to others becomes a central part of our true purpose. Don't you get that incredible feeling when you give to others? This is one of the ways to be truly ***X-traordinary***.

5. ***X-emplify*** the right thing

As humans, we're all guided by our moral compass. This is our internal set of principles — that inner conscience or a mirror. Our principles set us in the right direction and prevent us from going astray. Generally, they ensure that we stay in line with our expectations for ourselves. You might ask, why do we need these rules? The nice-to-have freedom of choice in what we want to do may not always match what we need to do.

To truly achieve the X Factor state where we X-hibit ***X-traordinary*** habits, we must ensure our inner compass stays consistent with our outward activities. We need to strive to model the right things as much as we humanly can. This may be further guided by our spirituality (connection to our Maker) and link directly to our purpose as it complements our passion and skills.

X-hibit That Little X-tra

It's the few X-tras we plug into our daily lives that give us the X-Factor and ensure we deploy those *X-traordinary* habits. In turn, those *X-traordinary* habits become normal via micro-steps and leveraging the cue-routine-reward habit loop cycle by Charles Duhigg. This loop is comprised of four aspects: cue, craving, response, and reward — a cue triggers your brain to do something, and this specific behaviour rewards you with a reward like dopamine surge.

A Personal Experience

A simple change in our vocabulary can create such an enormous shift in our achievements. I have seen this happen multiple times and right now, I'm extremely cautious about just saying 'No' to myself as an indicator of delivery. I would rather tell myself 'Not Yet' and ensure my 'work-in progress' is aligned to delivering on the task. It works like magic almost every single time.

I once took on a project in a field where I had little or no legacy knowledge. I really had to deploy the 'Not-Yet' mindset as I had lots to learn and simultaneously, I needed to achieve early wins as fast as possible! The first thing I did was to 'micro-step' this by breaking down the enormous task that appeared daunting into relatively small, actionable steps. The idea was that if I could make the steps small enough, they'd become too small to fail. This corresponds to research that revealed starting small makes new habits more likely to stick.

I held myself accountable to ensuring that the act of 'micro-stepping' happened consistently, in the right direction, and in a complementary fashion, like a set of Lego building blocks with each constituting a support to the other. This became a system for me, and I could see my capabilities grow to outpace my skill set needs on the project. At the same time, I was able to show early wins as I had split the project delivery milestones into actionable mini goals and would show visuals depicting milestone progress with my stakeholders.

I identified a 3-point road map that guaranteed my micro-stepping actions; coupled with my 'Not Yet' mindset this enabled me to achieve project delivery:

1. Understanding why I was up for the project itself.
2. Engaging in deliberate practice to accelerate my capability levels and maintain high level performance.
3. Establishing an accountability system.

I overdelivered on my project expectations but more importantly, I found a way to micro-step into goal achievements with the *'Not Yet'* mindset.

What Did We Learn?

This section of the book enabled us to understand how motivation gets built up and sustained. You also got to understand how the Underdog perceives 'No' as the '**N**ext **o**pportunity' and how this ultimately cumulates in the 'Not Yet' Mindset, which is the foundation that makes the Underdog truly unstoppable.

Next Steps

The next page contains a simple exercise that can help us assess an example of an event which may result in a 'No'. The idea is to walk through three simple steps that will enable us transition from the 'No' phase to the 'Not Yet' phase by adopting the 'Not Yet' Mindset. This is a very simple exercise that can become a potent way to reorient our thinking in the right way and achieve our expected goals.

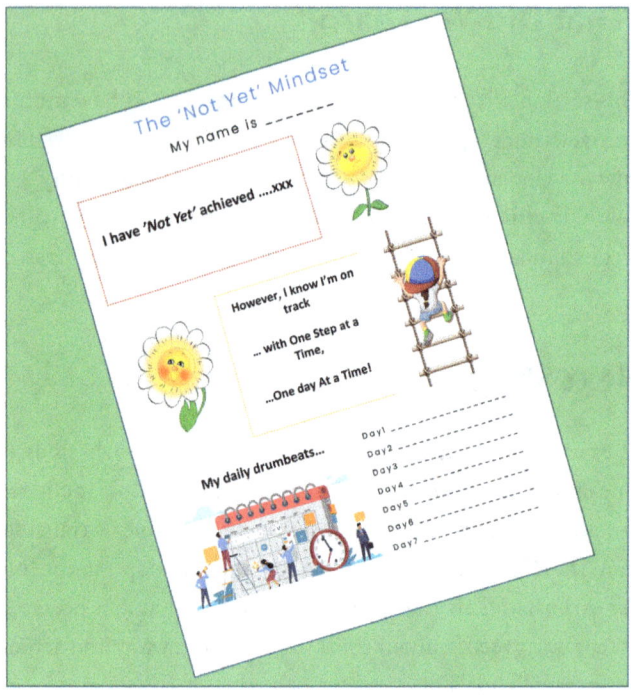

The Not Yet Mindset

To Leverage the Not Yet Mindset and thus turn around our perception of what isn't done yet to what is very much on track to getting done, we need to visualize things.

Step One: Highlight that one key activity which isn't yet done and which stresses you out each time you think about it.

Step Two: Re-iterate to yourself that even though the task or activity isn't concluded, it's work in progress and you know it takes one step at a time daily to achieve it.

Step Three: Literally callout in brief, these activities you need to close out on a daily beat to achieve it.

If you forget anything in the last chapter …

don't forget this:

'NO Is Simply Next Opportunity, Meaning — Not Yet'

CONCLUSION: THE UNDERDOG STAYS HUNGRY

'The Wolf on the hill is not as hungry as
the wolf climbing the hill'.

— Arnold Schwarzenegger

As individuals, we have all enjoyed different levels of privileges in our lives. Some have had great privileges and were 'born with a silver spoon in their mouth'. For others, it was a struggle from birth. This book about the Underdog aims to unpack the incredibly powerful ammunition we all have, which, more often than not, appears as a disadvantage. As you would've observed reading through the book, these building blocks constitute the Underdog's untold advantages. The Underdog's advantages are available to everyone and at every point of our respective journeys. In one instance, the Underdog Code can be used by those aiming to rise the ranks, as it enables them to accelerate even faster; in another instance, it can be used by those at the top in order to keep re-inventing themselves and to stay ahead of their game.

I'm convinced that by applying these codes (and not just reading them!) you will see substantial improvement across your endeavours. This will be possible as long as you stay directed by your values and not by your circumstances. Be careful not to jump into the river and get swept away by the currents as fighting the currents will make you lose control, negatively affecting your endeavours.

Stay focused and remember once again ...

> 'Where focus goes, energy flows'
>
> — Tony Robbins

One Last Exercise

Let's take a scenario in your life that didn't work out the way you wanted it to. What would you do now if you knew you could not fail?

- Write down 5 things that you would do as opposed to what you did.
- What belief barriers would you break? Write them down.

CONCLUSION: THE UNDERDOG STAYS HUNGRY

- Question the authenticity of these beliefs and mirror back the barriers positively, with supportive data.

This will turn your pain into your propane.

Above all, remind yourself day by day that success is made up of small incremental improvements, not necessarily big leaps. To truly enjoy the process is to build a sustainable pathway to success and this can only be done by focusing on, and *enjoying*, the process, rather than only the outcome.

Do reach out to share your progress with me as you deploy the Underdog Code. I would like to hear from you if you have any questions or need further assistance.

You may reach out to me at imomazin.com or SMS on +971 545 500 4800.

> Stay Amazing — Say to Yourself *I'm o-mazin*!

If you forget anything in this concluding chapter ...

don't forget this:

'The Underdog Mindset Is All You Need to Consistently Win!'

FURTHER READING AND RESOURCES

Introduction
Kim, W. C., & Mauborgne, R. (2005). *Blue ocean strategy: How to create uncontested market space and make the competition irrelevant.* Harvard Business School Press.

Chapter 2: Big Picture — Prepare for a Mindset Shift
Ferriss, T. (2007). *The 4-Hour Workweek: Escape 9-5, Live Anywhere, and Join the New Rich.* Crown Publishing Group.

Chapter 3: The Power of Perception — How Your Outlook Can Change Your Outcome
Canfield, J. (2021). *Visualization Techniques to Affirm Your Desired Outcomes: A Step-by-Step Guide.*

Thomson, G. and Macpherson, F. (2017), *Adelson's checkershadow illusion' in F. Macpherson (ed.).* The Illusions Index.

Adelson, E. H. (2000). *Lightness Perception and Lightness Illusions, The New Cognitive Neurosciences*, M. Gazzaniga (Ed). 2nd ed. pp. 339-351, MIT Press: Cambridge MA.

Adelson, E. H. 2005, *Checkers Shadow Illusion*. http://web.mit.edu/persci/people/adelson/Checkers Shadow_description.html MIT Website.

Zohuri, B. (2018). ***Physics of Cryogenics, First Law of Thermodynamics***. https://www.sciencedirect.com/topics/chemistry/first-law-of-thermodynamics#:~:text=The%20First%20Law%20of%20Thermodynamics%20states%20that%20energy%20cannot%20be,from%20one%20form%20to%20another.

Chapter 4: Who in the World Is an Underdog?

Zelazko, A. (2022). ***Encyclopaedia Britannica***. https://www.britannica.com/biography/Wilma-Rudolph.

Goldschmied, N. (2005). The Underdog Effect: Definition, Limitations, and Motivations. Why Do We Support Those at a Competitive Disadvantage? Graduate Theses and Dissertations. https://scholarcommons.usf.edu/etd/2899.

Judah, T. (2008). Bikila: Ethiopia's Barefoot Olympian. London: Reportage Press.

Maraniss, D. (2008). Rome 1960: The Olympics That Changed the World. New York: Simon and Schuster. ISBN 9781416534075. OCLC 214066042.

Kitun, S. & Fiske, S. (2022). *How Netflix turned a humble beginning into one of the most disruptive companies of the past hundred years.* https://technori.com/2019/09/18104-netflix-co-founder-marc-randolphs-new-memoir/admin/.

Baxter, K. (2022). *How underdog Morocco became 'the Rocky of this World Cup' and has uplifted a region.* Los Angeles Times, Dec 2022. https://www.latimes.com/sports/soccer/story/2022-12-12/world-cup-underdog-morocco-france-semifinal.

Walter, B. (2008). *Scotichronicon:Bks.XI-XII. Volume 6 of Scotichronicon: In Latin and English.* Aberdeen University Press, 1987. The University of Michigan. *Scotichronicon.*

Wikipedia (2022). Battle of Stirling Bridge. http://en.wikipedia.org/wiki/Battle_of_Stirling_Bridge.

Jacopo Della Quercia. (2010). *The 6 Most Insane Underdog Stories in the History of Battle The 6 Most Insane Underdog Stories in the History of Battle.* Cracked.com.

Nurmohamed, S. (2020). *Leading Teams: The Upside of Being an Underdog.* Harvard Business Review https://hbr.org/2020/01/the-upside-of-being-an-underdog.

Wheeler, K. (2021). *11 Underdog Brands That Differentiated Themselves From the Competition.* HubSpot https://blog.hubspot.com/marketing/brands-that-differentiated-themselves-from-the-competition.

Statista. (2022). *Consumer Goods & FMCG, Food & Nutrition The leading ice cream brands of the United States in 2022*. Sales **(in million US dollars)**.

https://www.statista.com/statistics/190426/top-ice-cream-brands-in-the-united-states/.

Chapter 5: The Underdog Doesn't Play Fair

Gladwell, M. (2013). *David and Goliath: Underdogs, Misfits, and the Art of Battling Giants*. First Edition. Little, Brown and Company.

Gladwell, M. (2014). *How David Beats Goliath*. Wayback Machine. Newyorker.com. 4 May 2009.

May, K.T. (2013). *TEDBlog — Culture TEDTalks David, Goliath and the appeal of the underdog: A Q&A with Malcolm Gladwell on this often-misunderstood story.* https://blog.ted.com/david-goliath-and-the-underdog-a-qa-with-malcolm-gladwell/.

Murphy Jr., B. (2014). *Three Things People Get Wrong About David vs. Goliath*. Inc. Newsletter. May 6th, 2014. https://www.inc.com/bill-murphy-jr/3-things-people-get-wrong-about-david-vs-goliath.html.

Chapter 6: The Underdog Pivots

Glazer, A. (2020). *How to Pivot in your Career and Life According to an Empowerment Coach.* Create & Cultivate

Aug 24th, 2020. https://www.createcultivate.com/blog/how-to-pivot-in-your-career-and-life/.

Chapter 7: The Underdog Has the 'Not Yet' Mindset

Enang, I. (2022). *Not Yet ... Mindset: Where Momentum Lives*. Imomazin Inc Feb 24th, 2022. https://imomazin.com/not-yet-mindset-where-momentum-lives/.

Enang, I. (2022) *'X'Factor: X-traordinary Habits*. Imomazin Inc March 3rd, 2022. https://imomazin.com/xfactor-x-traordinary-habits/.

Duhigg, C., (2013) The Power of Habit. Random House Books.

Notes

www.ingramcontent.com/pod-product-compliance
Lightning Source LLC
Chambersburg PA
CBHW071456080526
44587CB00014B/2129